Awake To Wildlife

D1593825

THE COMPLETE NATURALIST'S
Great Lakes Wildlife Almanac

Awake To Wildlife

The Complete Naturalist's
Great Lakes Wildlife Almanac

By Tim Nowicki

Production and design by Pegg Legg Publications
Editing by Tim Richard
All nature drawings by Tim Nowicki
Cover design and additional art by Dan Jacalone

Published by **Glovebox Guidebooks Publishing Company**
P.O. Box 852
Clarkston, MI 48347
To order 1-800-289-4843

Library of Congress

Nowicki, Tim, 1950 -

Awake To Wildlife
Great Lakes Wildlife Almanac
By Tim Nowicki (Glovebox Guidebooks)
ISBN 1-881139-06-9

Printed in the United States of America

10 9 8 7 6 4 3 2 1

To my parents, Lorraine and Norbert Nowicki,

They never discouraged
my interest in the natural world
and provided opportunities for its exploration.

Acknowledgments

Thankfully people like to see environments that are suitable for wildlife. Whether they were created or left undisturbed by the land owner or maintained by a state or municipality, these are the areas where urbanites, suburbanites and ruralites can still enjoy wildlife of many diverse forms.

These areas and people who enjoy them were often the inspiration for articles collected in this book. Many people enjoying these areas through the years have been curious enough to ask questions that I tried to answer in my articles. My thanks to those who asked the questions that helped guide me to subjects people found interesting.

While writing for the Observer & Eccentric Newspapers for the past 10 years, I have enjoyed working with two editors whose talents were greatly appreciated. Tim Richard said yes when I first suggested writing a nature column for the newspapers. He offered suggestions for topics, provided insight into writing and added spark to my articles. Sue Rosiek has reviewed my work and added her editorial expertise to make it as readable as possible.

Chuck Barnes from the Lloyd A. Stage Outdoor Education Center in Troy, Mich., reviewed the manuscript for any natural history concepts or facts that I may have misrepresented. His knowledge of natural history is hard to surpass, but if something is misrepresented, I take full responsibility. Colleagues, like Chuck, and the staff at the Independence Oaks Nature Center - Kathy

Thomas, Kathleen Dougherty and Lynn Conover, have provided invaluable information, discussions and observations through the years.

As in most people's lives, there are many strings attached to us pulling in all directions. My family has provided some wonderful insight and inspiration into the value of the natural world. But it takes time to put those ideas on paper. Doris, my wife, kept those strings from pulling in my direction when I needed to write the articles represented. Two of those strings, my daughter, Janice, and my son, Michael, have allowed me to see the world from a sometimes forgotten perspective.

T.N.

Contents

Spring

Summer

Autumn

Winter

Awake To Wildlife

Wildlife and the natural world are becoming more and more a part of everyone's life these days. More people are birding, feeding birds, and photographing wildlife than ever before. As our society becomes more mechanized, more regimented and stressful, people realize that the natural world offers a retreat from the everyday routine.

Casual walks through forest or field allow one to see a part of our world that is very different from what we encounter in man's artificial world. This change of environment can be very relaxing and therapeutic in many ways. I had a police chief take a class I taught because it provided a way for him to relieve his stress.

Even a bird feeder in the backyard can provide a diversion from everyday stress and serve as a constant source of entertainment. There always seems to be some activity to watch, bright colors to observe and new species to look for. This is where many people get started enjoying wildlife.

When our children were growing up, we had their high chair next to the window where they could see the bird feeder. Whenever a blue jay or cardinal would fly in to feed, either my wife or I would alert our children to their arrival. While our children were growing up they enjoyed the flashy colors and the movement of the birds as they flew in. I think because my daughter had heard the word blue jay so often, one of her first words was blue jay.

Exposing young people to the natural world is a wonderful gift that can last forever. Allowing children to explore, and beginning to saturate that sponge of curiosity, are not only gratifying to the child, but can be very enlightening to the supervising adult. As a child investigates the colors of fallen leaves, the texture of mullein leaves, the smell of sassafrass, or the sound of a cardinal, we all learn with the child.

A child has that insatiable sense of wonder that adults should never loose. Life for a young child is always interesting because everything he or she finds is new. We all enjoy the thrill of discovery when we encounter something new and interesting. That feeling can be experienced many times if we awake to wildlife. There is always wildlife around if we take the time to

As a child investigates the colors of fallen leaves or hears the sound of a cardinal, we all learn with the child.

look and observe. It can be found in your house, around your house, in the neighborhood, up state, down state, across the country and around the world.

Your yard is a good place to start watching wildlife. It can provide you with the opportunity to hone your observational skills. As wildlife is encountered, questions as to what the animal is, where it came from, what is it doing, whether it will stay, how many are there, or any number of other inquires will be raised. Each species you encounter does not require a trip to the library or time spent with the encyclopedia, but observant people, who are naturally curious, think about those kinds of things.

Learning about the animal being observed adds so much to your enjoyment. Looking at the color of a hummingbird or the flight of a dragonfly can be interesting in and of itself, but the more you learn about these things, the more interesting they become. E.O. Wilson says, "Our sense of wonder grows exponentially: the greater the knowledge, the deeper the mystery, and the more we seek knowledge to create new mystery."

Examining the skills and abilities of animals creates intrigue and awe. Just as we are enthralled by the mastery of a professional, the adaptations of animals are just as fascinating. Though they have different ways of adapting to their world, they are subject to the same environmental factors and physical factors that you and I are subject to. As we learn more about animals, we realize that we do things remarkably similarly to the way they do things.

One attraction of watching wildlife is that it can be done anywhere and at any time. People in offices have installed bird feeders in their view so they can enjoy its activities. Office workers in downtown Detroit and Grand Rapids search the sky for a peregrine falcon as they walk down the street to lunch. Even while in the car people can observe wildlife (making sure traffic is clear first!). I remember watching a kestrel flying parallel with my car on Jefferson Avenue in Detroit within sight of the Renaissance Center. After a moment or two, it flew across both lanes of traffic, in front of my car, and captured a mouse on the sidewalk.

There is no closed season for watching wildlife as there is for hunting or fishing. Take the time to enjoy the natural world any time of the year. Each season brings new and different challenges to spark that sense of wonder. Walking foot trails just for the exercise and the possibility of sighting wildlife is as valid a reason for being in the natural world as a hunter has when stalking a pheasant or an angler bobbing a hook and a worm in a lake.

Throughout the years, my personal experiences around our house, with family members, on the way to work, while walking local trails, or by traveling in the Great Lakes area have provided inspiration for my articles published in the Observer & Eccentric

Newspapers. I have tried to alert people to the never ending wonders that can be found in everyday life and to challenge and encourage others to enjoy those same experiences. My background and education allow me to interpret and identify some of these observations so you can understand the relevance, importance and fascination of such an observation.

Awakening to the wildlife around you can be extremely satisfying. Once you become aware of the diversity of life that surrounds you and to the marvels of that diversity, it will undoubtedly lead to an appreciation of all life forms. And as Baba Dioum said, "In the end, we will conserve only what we love, we will love what we understand, we will understand only what we are taught."

The natural world is a great teacher if we take the time to look, listen and observe what it has to say.

Providing nest material for birds.

Spring Nest Building

For eons now, winter has merged into spring as days lengthen, and temperatures slowly rise. Warm weather may not come at exactly the same time each year, but in time spring will melt into summer.

This predictability in climate has been ingrained in the behavior of all species of animals inhabiting the Midwest. They begin raising and feeding young in spring because the warm months ahead provide abundant food and mild temperatures. Those that start early enough generally get to raise more young.

Birds that build a nest to raise their young expend a great deal of energy in this endeavor. Some suburban yards are so well manicured that it is hard for a robin to find any dried grasses or mud to use as nest material. So in order to help the various species of birds nesting in your yard, why not supply some natural materials for them to use?

When you place concentrated sources of nesting material in your yard, birds will not have to spend as much time searching for suitable material. This allows them to get down to the business of egg laying and incubation sooner. It will also provide you with an opportunity to watch them gather the material, and possibly to watch them build the nest.

Dried grasses may be accumulated into a wire mesh cage similar to that used for a suet feeder. Material will not blow away and yet the birds will be able to see it. Do not hide it from their view, or your view.

If you have a long haired dog, put some of the hair you comb out into a similar wire mesh. In one museum, 78 percent of the nests examined contained animal hair. Most birds use it to line the cup of the nest which is in direct contact with the nestlings.

Some birds, like robins and barn swallows, use mud in their nest construction. Providing a shallow puddle with a dirt bottom can help these species to complete their nest. A readily available source can be very handy if you are a barn swallow that has been known to make 1,200 trips to get mud for a single nest.

Extra pieces of yarn or string can also be used by birds. Do not, however, put out yarn or string that is bright in color. Hot pink yarn or lemon yellow string, if incorporated into a nest could attract a predator. Birds can see color very well and a nest that is not camouflaged may easily be spotted by a crow or a hawk.

SOME SUBURBAN YARDS ARE SO WELL MANICURED THAT IT'S HARD FOR A ROBIN TO FIND ANY GRASSES OR MUD TO USE AS NEST MATERIAL.

Remember, if you want to attract wildlife to your yard, provide them with the three basic necessities of all living things: food, shelter and water. Nesting material is a great help if there is sheltered vegetation they can build a nest in.

Paddling To Nature

Water is one of those essentials for life. No living thing can exist without it. So exploring for wildlife near water can yield many experiences. But how do we get by the water to explore?

There are many ways to enjoy water - skiing, wind surfing, sailing and power boating - but canoeing is the water sport for the nature lover. A canoe is designed to allow travel in both shallow and deep water.

Poking along the shoreline of a lake or river is a good way to see wildlife. Each bend in the river can arouse that sense of discovery. Wildlife does not seem to distinguish the human form in a canoe as readily as it does outside the canoe. This allows closer encounters with those animals often associated with water and wetlands.

Turtles basking on a log will watch from a safe, but closer, distance as a canoe drifts by. Closer examination will enable identification of the "smiling" Blanding's turtle. A Blanding's turtle is a basker that has a yellow throat contrasting with a dark upper jaw. Where the two join a "smile" is created. Those turtles with a colorful yellow striped head and red bordering its shell are the painted turtles.

Several species of ducks and geese can be seen from a canoe. In late summer male ducks, like mallards and wood ducks, are colored like females of their species. The bright, colorful feathers of breeding males are no longer needed, and so they grow a

camouflaged set like the females for protection.

A canoe can get into hidden backwater areas where animals seek seclusion. Great blue herons often hunt in these backwaters so they will be undisturbed. If you come upon one, it will probably squawk as it takes flight. When they begin flight their large wings, spanning six feet, will wooosh the air, their long legs will trail behind, and their necks will gradually tuck back on their "shoulders" and come to rest in an "S" shape. This "S" shape neck position is characteristic of all herons, bitterns and egrets while in flight. It separates them from the long-legged, long-necked cranes. Cranes fly with their necks stretched straight forward.

Silent paddling often treats the canoeist to a symphony of sounds. A little yellow, black-masked warbler can often be seen singing *whichy whichy* from the stalks of cattails. Common yellowthroats make a loud sound for a five-inch long bird.

If you hear the sound of an old treadle sewing machine, it's not a tailor making a suit, it's the sound of the marsh wren in the rushes. More often heard than seen, this five-inch-long, brown colored bird seeks the shelter of the tall plants along the shoreline.

As you scan the shoreline for wildlife, it will be hard not to see some of the beautiful wildflowers that like the wet soil. One that is easily seen from a canoe is the scarlet red cardinal flower that blooms in mid-summer. Be sure to stop and examine the flower, but be cautious of poison ivy that may also be growing nearby.

Highway Hawks

Almost everyone these days drives on the expressways because they are great ways to cover a lot of ground in a short time. But along the expressways there are fields, forests, fences and telephone poles and these four factors are the reasons we see so many red-tailed hawks.

Hawk watching is a great pasttime for expressway travelers. Once a few basic techniques are reviewed, it's easy to spot them at 60 mph. Red-tailed hawks are the most common species of hawk seen along the expressways. They stand 22 inches tall in an upright position. They also have a white breast. There are some streaks on the breast, but they are difficult to see from a distance. A hawk's upright position, white breast and brown back will distinguish it from a crow, which is black and perches on an angle.

In order to develop "hawk eyes," begin looking for unusual extensions on the top of telephone poles. Scan the tops of a series of telephone poles. If one has an extra extension, or protrusion, chances are good it's a hawk. Be sure to check the pine trees growing in the median. Hawks like to perch on top of them also. A white extension on a green pine will alert you to their presence.

In order to develop "hawk eyes" begin looking for unusual extensions on top of telephone poles.

Because hawks perch upright, they appear unusual when they sit on a tree branch. Their white breasts are lighter than the gray of a tree and contrast sharply enough to draw your attention.

My wife and I traveled with some friends along an expressway in eastern Michigan, during the month of February, on our way to do some cross country skiing. February is a good time to watch for hawks because there are no leaves to obstruct your view and the birds are pairing in preparation for nesting. Along the 42 mile stretch of expressway the four "hawk eyes" in the car counted 20 hawks on the way there and 29 hawks on the way back. That is an average of one hawk every two miles and every mile-and-a-half respectively.

Rural expressways are good places to watch for hawks but urban roads and freeways are also places to watch. All hawks and owls are protected by law, and over the past 30 years their numbers have increased. Some of the birds are now tolerating the presence of man and are nesting near urban developments. I have seen red-tailed hawks on the roofs of houses, hunting from metal light poles, and perched on the only tree in the area along a major secondary road in the city of Detroit.

Short grass along the expressways and roads allows hawks to see their prey more easily. Coupled with the abundance of suitable perches, it makes expressways excellent places to hunt. I have speculated about another possible advantage. Mice near the roadway are constantly in view of moving cars that pose no threat, as they have learned over time. Maybe mice become conditioned to the constant movement of the cars and are not as likely to react to a hawk moving through the air. Success rates of hawks hunting along expressways would have to be compared to those in similar habitats away from roads to determine if my supposition is correct.

When hawks hunt so close to expressways there is also the chance that they will come in conflict with automobiles. I have seen red-tailed hawks dead on the side of the road, just as I see raccoons, skunks and opossum. One day I saw exactly how a hawk's death can occur. A hawk perched in a tree on the outside shoulder of the road took flight after it spotted prey across the road near the median. With its eyes intently focused on the prey, the hawk flew about three feet above the road across both lanes. I came within a fraction of a second of hitting it.

Before the leaves of trees emerge, look for the nests of hawks. Hawks build a flat topped structure made primarily of twigs. Leafy, globular structures are squirrel nests. One of the best ways to spot nests is to look into a woodlot with the sun backlighting the trees. This will allow you to see any large black objects in the branches. While you are looking for hawk nests, check the nest and see if there is a head protruding. It could be a great horned owl.

If you find an active hawk nest do not disturb it; they will abandon their nest if disturbed. Enjoy the opportunity to watch the pair as they add material to the nest and hunt for food.

Mayapples And Moths

Scientists have been able to identify many of the basic principles of nature. Animal camouflage, habitat preference, succession, and territory are just some of those principles. A basic knowledge of these principles is very helpful when observing the natural world.

But basic principles are just that: basic. Most of these principles are manifest in many different ways in various plants and animals. For instance, numerous research projects have illustrated the unique ways in which camouflage is achieved. Crab spiders that rely on quickness and patience, and not a web for catching food, are able to change from white to yellow, depending on the color of the flower they are on. Frogs typically found on the forest floor are not green, but brown and black - to match the dried leaves they hide among.

One spring I discovered an interesting way a moth protects itself from predators during the day. While examining the spring wildflower mayapple, I was surprised to see several moths resting on the downward facing flower. It took me by surprise, because I did not notice them at first. Their creamy white coloration blended in perfectly with the shaded white petals of the blossom. Though the blossom is only two to two-and-a-half inches across, there were as many as five moths positioned like petals around the flower.

A mayapple with a moth.

Those creamy white moths were identified to be white slant lined moths. I do not know if they had been feeding on the flower during the night and then just settled on the edge when daylight came, or if they always come to this flower for protection when it is in bloom.

No matter what the reason, they were very well hidden. The palm tree/umbrella like leaves of mayapple completely cover the flower when viewed from above. That, in combination with their petal like coloration, complete with a slant line on the wings to match the break between petals, would surely camouflage them from potential predators.

Next time you walk by some mayapples, see if you can find white slant lined moths.

WATCHING THE
EAGLES DANCE

Bald eagles are not a common sight in the southern Great Lakes area, but encounters with this species are increasing.

In 1988 one adult was spotted in December during the Detroit Audubon Society Christmas Bird Count. A couple years after that, two separate observers called the Detroit Audubon Society office to report seeing a bald eagle on I-75 near 12 Mile Rd. just outside the city of Detroit. Near Detroit Edison's nuclear power plant in Monroe, Michigan, there has been a nesting pair of eagles during the late 1980s and early 1990s.

In the mid 1980's, while watching my daughter at a playground, I looked up and saw what looked like a bald eagle high overhead. Despite its altitude, I could tell it was a large bird. Its white head and tail blended with the light blue of the sky, and all I could really define were the two large wings. It was undoubtedly a migrant heading south for the winter.

Any species of eagle is impressive. Their size and power are evident in their feet and bill. Even non-birders enjoy the opportunity to see eagles, particularly when they are in the wild.

In the spring of 1992, while with a group at Ottawa National Wildlife Refuge east of Toledo on US-2, I had a chance to see three eagles within 45 minutes. One person in our group spotted a "hawk" in the distance. When I looked at it initially I thought it was too large for a hawk that far away. After a closer examination my suspicion was verified. It was not a hawk, rather an eagle.

By this time everyone was watching the bird through binoculars and noticed a second bird approaching the first one. There was a noticeable difference in size between the two birds. Males are smaller and females are larger. These eagles were not adults; they did not display the white head and tail of the mature birds four to five years old.

As we watched, they suddenly approached each other and grabbed talons. One bird was upside down while the other approached from the top. Once they grabbed hold of each other's feet they began to fall. They started high in the sky and then with tangled talons tumbled and tumbled downward out of control for several seconds until they went out of sight below the tree top horizon.

They started high in the sky and then with tangled talons tumbled and tumbled downward out of control.

We did not see any sign of the birds until several moments later. Then one bird rose above the horizon and started flying at tree top level in our direction. In a short time the bird was only 50 yards away flying in plain view of the entire group.

This display of aerial acrobatics was probably a prelude to serious courtship. We felt very fortunate to have been in the field at the right time to have experienced such an event.

An early spring meadowlark.

Early Spring
Meadowlarks

A familiarity with the natural world allows one to predict upcoming events with reasonable accuracy. Discounting the predictable change of season, within each season there is a sequence of events.

The arrival of red-winged blackbirds to cattails along the edge of roadways and other marshy areas is expected on the first warm days in March. It warms the heart to see a friend who has been away for several months return to their summer home.

First encounters of spring arrivals are always an enjoyable experience because they foretell that the consistency and stability of nature prevail.

Meadowlarks are also one of those early spring arrivals. They can often be seen flying along the sides of expressways or in the median separating the roadways.

Even when one is traveling at 55 mph, it is easy to identify a meadowlark. One has to be alert for traffic, but if a light brown-backed bird, with bright yellow underparts interrupted by a black necklace, flies by, it is going to be a meadowlark. Also look for white outer tail feathers and its shallow wingbeats. As their name implies, meadowlarks are typically found in open grassy areas and are about the size of a robin.

Midwest states actually have two species of meadowlark. Eastern meadowlarks predominate, but western meadowlarks can also be found in similar habitats. In the field their plumages look very similar. However, when they sing it is easy to distinguish each species. Western meadowlarks have a much sweeter, flute-like song compared to the harsh sound produced by the eastern meadowlark.

Both species arrive from their wintering grounds in the southern states about the same time as their blackbird relatives. Though they are not very black like many other blackbirds, several body structures, such as the bill, have caused scientists to group them together. Northern orioles, that will be returning soon, are closely related to grackles, cowbirds and red-wings in the blackbird family.

Meadowlarks frequently perch on fence poles. They will often stand very erect while extending their heads upward and sing to proclaim their territory. A word phrase that simulates the phrasing of the song is *Spring of the Year*.

If you get a chance to watch "Gunsmoke" reruns, listen for the song of the western meadowlark as they ride across the plains. If you cannot watch any reruns, at least take note of the meadowlarks as you ride along the expressways.

Meadowlarks frequently perch on fence poles. They will stand very erect while extending their head upward and proclaim their territory.

Watching A Spring Fox Hunt

As I entered I-275 in the western suburbs of Detroit one day I saw a red fox in a clearing near the entrance ramp. I stopped on the ramp and from inside my car observed the fox. A car serves as an excellent blind from which to view wildlife. Animals cannot see the human outline and thus are not as easily frightened.

With the aid of my binoculars, I was able to watch its head movements as it searched in holes and hiding places for prey items. Red fox, one of two species of fox found in Michigan and the Midwest in general, have a varied diet. Their omnivorous diet and nocturnal habits enable them to survive in suburban areas, if they can avoid the freeway funeral.

During winter they feed on small rodents, rabbits and carrion. In summer, they will supplement their diet with insects and berries.

When this fox began hunting in the ditch near the fence that borders expressways, I got out of my car and approached on foot. It was so busy concentrating on finding food that it was unaware of my presence.

My view through the binoculars made it appear like it was only 10 yards away. After a short time, it walked down the ditch and out of sight.

Red fox are most active at night, but if food is scarce, they may have to extend their hunting schedule. The added pressure of a litter of pups may have forced this fox to hunt during the day.

Five pups are born, on the average, during March and April and put an additional burden on the adults to procure food.

Adult fox may travel five miles a night in search of food. In Michigan, the area where a fox is found - its home range - is roughly 955 acres. Within this area, adult fox will find food, dig an underground den (or enlarge an abandoned woodchuck den), raise young and defend the area from other fox.

Fox were not very common in heavily forested areas before the lumbering era. After the large tracts of pine, and hardwood forests were cleared, scrub lands, meadows and fields developed, which are prime habitats for red fox.

Their numbers increased because of man's interference. It is ironic that the hand of man is now destroying the fox's habitat where the tracks of a bulldozer can be seen overunning the cat-like tracks of the fox.

Snipe Hunting For
Woodcocks

Whenever I get a chance, I try to explore natural areas and things around me. One day, my wife and I invited some friends over for dinner and asked them if they would be interested in birdwatching afterwards.

I was almost going to tell them we would be going "snipe hunting" but, instead, decided to tell them we would be searching for a courting woodcock.

Many people know the woodcock as a chunky, brown, upland game bird with a long narrow bill. It is found in wooded areas most of the time but is actually related to shorebirds like sandpipers,

A male woodcock in flight.

plovers and snipes.

They spend the winter months in such southern states as Louisiana. Then in the spring, like many other birds, they return north to nest and raise young.

After a delicious lasagna dinner, we drove to the field areas near an apartment complex where I had watched them perform their ceremonial courtship display for the past five years.

I was almost certain the birds would be there again this spring, but I wanted to be sure before I brought my class there to see them.

At sunset, or a little after, almost like clockwork, a male entered the sandy, open area surrounded by cottonwood and box elder trees. We knew when he entered because he started his *BEEEENT* call while on the ground.

Darkness and field vegetation prevented us from seeing the

bird, but we could hear his calls gradually increase to about once every 10 or 20 seconds.

The male continued to call for a short time while still on the ground. Then, when the calling stopped, we watched the backlit horizon to the west in hopes of seeing the bird fly up.

On his very first flight, he passed right in front of us, only about 10 feet over our heads - close enough so we could see his three-inch long bill.

The clear sky allowed us to watch the bird gain altitude until he was a speck, barely visible in the sky, directly over the area he was calling from on the ground. Chorus frogs and spring peeper frogs calling from nearby ponds almost drowned the high pitched twittering sound produced by the male in flight.

His outer wing feathers are narrower than the female's, which causes the twittering sound as the air passes over them while flying.

THE MALE'S OUTER WING FEATHERS ARE NARROWER THAN THE FEMALE'S, WHICH CAUSES THE TWITTERING SOUND WHILE FLYING.

After a minute flight, the male woodcock began to come back to earth. We could barely see his descent, but we could tell he was coming down by the *kissing* sound he produced until shortly before his landing.

He returned to the same general area where we first heard him calling. This is the area to which he wants to attract a female for mating.

The same sequence of events and combination of sounds will be repeated until the darkness of night. Some birds also perform this ceremony in the morning around sunrise - all for the purpose of perpetuating the species.

Our friends thanked us for an unusual evening's entertainment.

Daytime Woodchucks

Mowed areas along freeways and open fields in the country are good places to spot Michigan's largest squirrel, the woodchuck.

To many of us, this animal is known as a groundhog. To the scientific community, it's *Marmota monax*.

No matter what you call it, this mammal, big enough to be seen readily in open fields from a moving car, measures about 18 inches in length and weighs about 10 pounds. From a distance, it looks like a brown mound of soil. But watch awhile, and you will see it begin to move.

Woodchucks are built low to the ground and are designed for digging burrows, which they use for resting and raising their young. On Feb. 2 everyone looks to see if Punxsutawney Phil in Pennsylvania will see his shadow when he emerges from his hibernation burrow.

How do we know it's Phil and not Phyllis?

Animals seen in grassy fields early in spring are males that have awakened from their winter rest and are beginning to feed again. Females will emerge later and begin to feed on grasses and plants that are starting to turn green. They will have to regain as much as 50 percent of the weight they lost during the winter.

Most mammals are nocturnal and are difficult to see under the cover of darkness. Woodchucks, however, are one of the few mammals active during the day. This behavior allows travelers the opportunity to see them as they motor along our expressways.

In early spring, before new grasses and ground covers emerge, woodchucks can be seen foraging on leaves in trees several feet off the ground. Most of the time woodchucks feed on low grasses, but occasionally they stand upright on their rear haunches. This behavior allows them to scan the area for potential predators. Native Americans call them "standing mice" because of this habit, while some call them "whistle pigs" because of a warning vocalization.

Although the woodchuck's large size reduces the number of potential predators, fox, coyote, dogs, and an occasional red-tailed hawk take their toll. Many are lost to the Goodyear and Firestone as well. Fields and vacant land where woodchucks live are being developed, and as a result, animals are being displaced to less preferred habitats.

Many people are seeing woodchucks in very urban and suburban areas where they were seldom seen before. They seem to be adapting to our lawns, gardens and decks with little difficulty. Given the necessity, many forms of wildlife can adapt to human habitats.

Next time you drive around town or along a freeway, see if you can spot a woodchuck grazing along the edge of a field.

Woodchucks are one of the few mammals active during the day. Look for them as you travel the expressways.

Dried Moss, Dog Hair And Chickadees

Spring is certainly the time of courtship and nest building for birds in the Great Lakes area. Many species that were feeding at your feeder during the winter are now preparing to raise young.

Chickadees live in family groups with mated pairs and unmated individuals. Within each group and within each sex of each group is a dominance hierarchy. The first pair to nest is the most dominant mated pair.

A group of black-capped chickadees attended our feeder all winter and made our yard part of their territory. So it was not surprising to find them nesting near our yard when spring arrived.

One day I watched a chickadee leave the feeder and fly to the ground where it began collecting moss from a slab of cement that was almost buried. This was the first time I had noticed any individuals collecting nest material.

I was too late to see where the bird went with its beakful of moss, but the next time a chickadee arrrived I paid particular attention. On the way back from our neighbor's yard, it landed in our magnolia tree and allowed me a moment to see that it had a beak full of dog hair.

This was an indication that the nest was near completion, because mammal hair is used to line the inner cup of the nest. In addition to collecting moss and mammal hair, chickadees use small, fine strips of bark and pieces of fern to build their nests.

From our magnolia, it flew to some of the maples in the yard next to us. I was barely able to see it until it flew again and entered a small hole in another maple tree. This hollow in the tree was made from the decaying of a branch that had broken off long ago. They may also use old woodpecker holes.

After the nest is complete, they begin laying four to eight eggs. When the last egg has been laid incubation will begin. Approximately 12 days later the sound of chirping nestlings may be heard inside the nest cavity.

A couple weeks later I slowly approached the nest hole to sneak a peek inside. As my head came near the hole, evidently casting a shadow inside the hole, I heard a hissing sound. It is believed that sounding like a snake or a large cavity dwelling mammal is their method of warding off potential predators. I was definately startled to hear a sound like that.

Piecing together some clues from careful observation of bird behavior can yield some rewarding experiences, even in your backyard.

Songs Of Spring

Warm temperatures and extended daylight hours in April and May have prompted our winter resident birds to begin courtship activities. Cardinals and titmice that come to feed at our feeder are actively singing in the yard at this time.

Males sing a song to announce to other males where the boundaries of their territory extend. It also serves to coordinate breeding activities with the female. Unlike most species of birds, female cardinals sing. In fact, they sing duets with males that sound like one bird singing.

Cardinals have a variety of songs, but one common song of a cardinal is a strong whistle-like *cheer cheer cheer*. Another one is a clear two syllable *pretty pretty pretty*. Since a cardinal's song can be heard for quite a distance, you will have to search the upper branches of the entire yard.

Another bird with a tuft on its head is the tufted titmouse. This kissing cousin to the black-capped chickadee sings a clear song reminiscent of the word phrase *Peter Peter Peter*.

A third tufted bird that comes to many feeders in a backyard is the blue jay. Like the cardinal, blue jays produce more than just one sound. Most of us are familiar with the *jay* call of the blue jay - that's how it got its name. But another vocalization of the blue jay sounds like a rusty pump handle being worked up and down.

> To help hear bird songs inside the house, try installing an inexpensive intercom outside by the feeder.

Listening to these songs in the morning certainly helps start the day right. To help hear those songs inside the house, try installing an inexpensive intercom.

A local electronics store sold a simple intercom for less than $10. We installed one end under the overhang of the house by the feeders facing toward the backyard, and threaded the wire through the storm windows into the kitchen to connect the other end.

When we want to listen, we turn on the switch and hear bird songs. It's surprising the distance from which we can hear their sounds. Not only does this system work well in early spring when the temperature is too cold to open the windows, it also allows my wife and me to communicate from the house to the backyard.

Up A Tree With A
Sreech Owl

Laying eggs and incubating in February may seem peculiar, but that is when great horned owls begin their nesting cycle. Screech owls nesting in southeastern Michigan begin their nesting in March or April.

Owls do not build their own nests. They use abandoned nests of squirrels, other birds, or hollows in trees. Since no other birds are nesting in winter, owls have their choice of nesting sites.

Young are ready to leave the nest by late May to early June. I have seen great horned owls in great blue heron nests when the herons arrive in spring. Their presence did not seem to bother the herons, which were intent on courting and preparing their own nests.

One year about the second week of May, while walking along the Rouge River, I found an old tree stump with an excavated hole in it. I felt there was activity inside because there were fresh scratch marks outside the hole, and every time I walked by, leaves inside the hole were in a different position.

Eventually one day I walked past the hole and saw the face of a young screech owl filling the opening. That verified my suspicions. Once I knew what was occupying the nest, I began looking for the adults nearby and on one occasion I saw one tucked under a tangle of grape vines. Not long after that, I saw one hugging the trunk of an adjacent tree - looking very much like a piece of bark.

When it was close to the time when those young would leave the nest I took my camera equipment one night to investigate the hole. When I arrived, an adult flew up to me and began calling from just a few feet above my head. This was a sure sign that there were young outside the nest.

When I looked around with my flashlight, I found a young owlet climbing the trunk of a tree. It hugged the trunk with its body and climbed with its claws. While one foot was in motion, the bill grabbed the bark for stabilization. Within a matter of minutes the young owl got to some branches that allowed it to jump from one to another and join its parents.

Upon leaving the nest cavity young screech owls probably fall to the ground like young wood ducks when they leave the nest. Since young owls cannot fly then, they must get off the ground and away from danger. The only way they could get to the upper branches was by climbing.

Nighttime can be an exciting time to explore the woods and fields. After all, most animals are nocturnal. Putting red cellophane over a flashlight will allow you to see, but not disturb, the animals.

Nighttime can be an exciting time to explore the woods. Putting red cellophane over a flashlight will allow you to see, but not disturb, the animals.

Those Ichneumon
Wasps

Walking through the woods in spring is marvelous. Temperatures are usually not too hot or too cold. Rain has not dampened our spirits. And insects have not become bothersome. Such perfect conditions have enabled those in the woods to walk leisurely and observe carefully such things as wildflowers blooming and emerging, birds singing and nesting along with frogs calling and mating.

A slow jaunt through the woods can yield some fascinating discoveries. For instance, as I was looking down at some large flowered trillium blooming by the trail, I noticed a wasp on a log. I identified it as a wasp because it had a narrow constriction between its thorax and abdomen. When I looked more closely, I saw it was a female ichneumon wasp laying eggs.

Ichneumon wasps lay their eggs on the larva of other insects, including other wasps. It is believed they can detect the vibrations of feeding larvae inside a log by sensors on their feet. They can also smell the larva with their antennae in order to be sure it's the correct larva species. In addition to antenna that are about half as long as their body, female ichneumons have a long filament extending from the end of their abdomen. This is called an ovipositer.

Some ichneumon wasps have ovipositers two or three times as long as their bodies. The ovipositer consists of three filaments: one

45

An ichneumon wasp on a log.

is hard and drill-like, the other two are soft and U-shaped to fit around the "drill." Once the proper larva has been located, the female positions her body so the ovipositer, when arched over her body, can be drilled through the wood and into the body of the larva where the egg is laid. All this is done through senses other than sight.

Different species of ichneumon wasps lay their eggs in different hosts. Some lay their eggs in the larva of cutworms that infest your garden. Another species will lay its eggs in tent caterpillars.

After an egg is laid, the wasp larva develops and lives inside its host. It will feed on the host without killing it and will remain inside the host until the pupa is just about ready to emerge as an adult.

Many species of ichneumon wasp are found in woods, but some are attracted to the lights of your home. They are orange-brown in color and about an inch long. If one should enter your house, don't be alarmed by a "stinger" that could "reach to the bone", try to release it unharmed because it will help reduce the insect pest population, as do other species of wasps and hornets.

Springtime Newborn

The reproductive cycle of animals in the Great Lakes area is timed so that young animals are born in spring or early summer. Young born at the beginning of the warm season when food is abundant, will have several months to grow and mature before winter. Cold temperatures and a lack of food make winter a very trying time for all animals, especially young of the year.

Though great horned owls, which begin nesting in late January and early February, may seem like an exception to the rule, their young leave the nest in May just in time for the mild temperatures and abundant food of summer.

White-tailed deer drop their fawns in late spring and early summer so they too will grow strong on mothers' milk and lush vegetation. Rut activities in fall allow time for the 200-day gestation period to be complete when food is more available. Winter can be hard on pregnant females, but it would be devastating on fawns.

Animals such as snakes, squirrels, and frogs that appear smaller than usual or expected are often thought to be baby animals. But many people are not aware of the diversity of species that can be found in our area and thus mistake new species for the babies of others.

Many who see a red squirrel for the first time think it is a baby squirrel. Red squirrels are only 12 inches long, compared to the familiar fox squirrel that is 20 inches long. There are several features that help separate one species from another, but size is the most striking first clue.

Those who walk along shallow pools of water in spring, and are observant enough to see a small chorus frog or spring peeper, will often call them baby frogs. This is a reasonable deduction because they are only about one-and-half inches long, far smaller than the five-inch leopard frog.

Small species are seldom seen and thus not readily recognized. A brown snake is not much bigger than a large earthworm and is often mistaken for a baby snake. Brown snakes have a black collar line behind the head, are generally no more than 12 inches long, and are about 3/8-inch in diameter. Since garter snakes are much larger and are most commonly seen, people do not associate an adult snake with being so thin and short.

There is a great deal of diversity in the natural world, and walking through fields and forests with a watchful eye will reward you with the small and seldom seen, but do not become confused because of its size.

Woolly Bears And Caterpillars

Woolly bear caterpillars may be a more appropriate topic for the fall season, but their presence in spring is what makes them unusual.

During fall, woolly bears are fairly common around neighborhoods, in fields and in woodlots. Many are moving quite fast for caterpillars and make one think that they know where they are going and that they are late. Though it may appear that they are moving rapidly, they are traveling at only .05 mile per hour.

They move fast in fall because cold weather is probably about

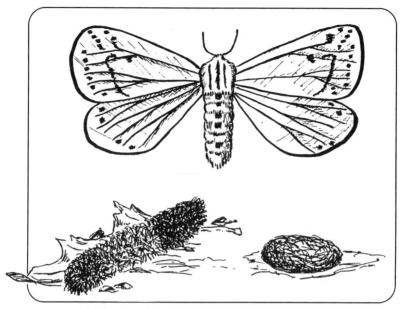

to set in. With the advent of cold weather, woolly bears look for a place to spend the winter. Under a rock, in a tree crevice, or any other secure place will do.

But instead of forming a cocoon like many moths, they overwinter as a caterpillar. Then in spring, when temperatures are warm enough, they awaken and search for food. Once they have fed, they search for a suitable place to form a cocoon.

It seems strange to see a caterpillar so early in the season. Even before the awakening of butterflies like mourning cloaks or tortoise shells that overwinter as adults, woolly bear caterpillars can be seen in the dried grasses of spring.

If you try to pick up one, you will be surprised how difficult it is. The hairs break off very easily when touched, causing it to slip from your fingers. This may be an adaptation that protects them from being eaten by a predator.

Following a light spring snack, the woolly bear finds a place to form a cocoon. In addition to silk used by caterpillars to form a cocoon, woolly bears weave in some of their long hairs. Most cocoons are made in April and May. Pupa remain in the cocoon for about two weeks.

If the typical reddish and black banded woolly bear formed the cocoon, an Isabella tiger moth will emerge. These moths are dull grayish and tawny yellow with some black dots on the wings. Females have approximately a 3-inch wingspan, while males have a 2-inch wingspan.

Other wooly looking caterpillars come in black and white, tan, black with a narrow red band, or white. Most of these species develop into moths with bold white stripes on their wings; hence, the name tiger.

Early April
Mourning Cloaks

One cool spring morning my students and I were watching a male mallard duck swimming in a pond at the University of Michigan-Dearborn's environmental study area. We were all exclaiming how beautiful the iridescent head was as it reflected the rays of morning sunshine.

I was so engrossed in watching the mallard that I almost stepped on a butterfly resting on the ground. The sun's rays had warmed this mourning cloak so it could begin searching for food.

This butterfly appeared to be sipping on the morning dew clinging to blades of grass. Sap seeping from wounds of a tree also provides water, but there is the added benifit of sugar in tree sap. Sugar found in sap or nectar is needed to supply energy for the active butterfly.

During winter months, the adult mourning cloak expends little energy because it has been hibernating under a rock or in the crevices of bark. Overwintering as an adult is unusual for butterflies. Most species spend the winter in the egg or chrysalis stage.

Another interesting feature of the mourning cloak is its ability to regulate its body temperature. Most insects are totally dependent on the temperature outdoors before they can become active. Warm weather is required before the body temperature of an insect rises sufficiently to allow it to move.

Mourning cloaks, however, are able to control their body temperature by positioning themselves perpendicular to the sun, angling their wings and shivering internally to generate heat. Like arctic butterflies, the wings of the mourning cloaks are dark colored next to their body. This helps absorb more warmth and allows transfer of that heat to the body muscles. They often select hibernation sites on the south side of a tree and will press their body against the bark to warm it through conduction.

> A feature of the mourning cloak is its ability to regulate its body temperature by positioning itself perpendcular to the sun.

Such behavior allows them to arise from their long winter rest very early in the spring when the temperature is still too cold for most insects.

Chances are good an early April butterfly is a mourning cloak. To be certain, look for a dark purple-brown color on top of the wings, bordered by a wide band of cream yellow along the outer edges. Just inside the cream border is a row of blue spots.

Another early butterfly is the spring azure, but it's active later in spring. Spring azures are an intense blue above and are only the size of a quarter - much smaller than the three-inch-wide mourning cloak.

Survival Skills

Many of the animals we see around our yards have capabilities that are quite extraordinary. Not just the ability to fly, or dig, or smell, but the ease and precision in which they perform these functions are remarkable.

Every time I watch the downy woodpecker fly toward the suet attached on the tree trunk, I am amazed. It will fly at such a rate that I can barely detect its approach. There are times when I think I have seen a bird arrive, but when it lands out of sight and stays there for several moments, I begin to doubt myself.

What amazes me is that at the appropriate instant, the woodpecker will "put on the brakes," change its body position from horizontal to vertical, grab hold of a suitable location, and perch without any disruption to its laser landing. There are times when it seems I should find its head protruding through the opposite side of the tree because it failed to pull up at the right moment.

I remember watching house sparrows flying directly toward a chain link fence without adjusting their elevation to fly over the fence. They did not change their speed of flight as they approached, they just folded their wings at the precise instant and darted through the opening. Once through, they continued their flight without the apparent lose of stride.

Squirrels tight-roping electrical and telephone wires always fascinate me, especially those crossing over a busy road. One false step and its "curtains for *Scurius*." Their ability to jump from flimsy

A squirrel tight-roping an electrical wire.

branch to a tenuous twig and to know how much exertion is needed has always puzzled me as well. They may not calculate correctly all the time, but most of the time they are right on target.

Watching the ruby-throated hummingbird hovering at a feeder and instantly adjusting its position either forward, up, down, right, left, or even backwards is remarkable to say the least.

No single animal has all these and other capabilities, but each animal has adaptations which allow it to survive in a very efficient manner.

SEEING THE SELDOM SEEN
Owl

Owls are one of the most widely recognized groups of birds. Their large, forward facing eyes, their facial pattern, and "ear" tufts of many species make them easily distinguished from other birds.

Many people can recognize an owl, but most people rarely if ever see one. If you have not seen an owl, then the months of April and May are the time to be on the lookout.

One sure way to see an owl is to find its nest. Owls like the great horned owl do not actually build their own nests. They use old, abandoned red-tailed hawk, crow, or even great blue heron nests. Some will nest in cavities formed from broken tree limbs, or on top of a sturdy squirrel nest. Nesting for owls begins in January and February, long before hawks or herons return to occupy nests they used previously.

In March, the young hatch and begin growing rapidly. Within a few weeks, the young are large enough to sit upright in the nest. This enables you to see them from a distance.

Nests used by owls are fairly large and can be seen from a distance when the trees are leafless. Large, flat-topped structures placed on main branches, or in the fork of main branches, can be recognized because they disrupt the usual form of the tree.

When a young bird or an adult pro-trudes above the top surface, you know the nest is active. Many nests can be spotted while you are driving along the expressway. Look toward the sun so the trees are backlighted and it will help to accentuate the large nest structure from the branching of the tree.

ONE SURE WAY TO SEE AN owl is TO find its NEST. THEy USE ABAN-doNEd REd-TAILEd hAwk, CROW, OR EVEN GREAT blUE HERON NESTS.

Great horned owls are one of the most commonly seen species in the Mid-west. They have adapted well to the patchy arrangement of the land. Fields interrupted by small woodlots make per-fect habitat for the red-tailed hawk and the great horned owl.

They have become tolerant of humans also. Many occupy nests within a 100 yards of an expressway, and I have seen one nesting within 75 yards of a subdivi-sion in southeast Michigan.

Another way to spot an owl is to watch for loud congregations of crows. Crows will call to collect others as they mob and pester an owl they found. Their calls are much louder and more vigorous than their usual vocalizations. If you locate the mob, your presence may cause the owl to fly. When it does, all the crows will take flight and chase it. The big, square headed one in the front of the flock is the owl.

Bird Displacement At The
Bird Feeder

Providing feeding stations for wildlife in your backyard is a great way to realize the diversity of life in the surrounding area. As different species use the feeders, pond or nest material provided, write down their names. After a few years you will be surprised how many different species you have seen.

Identifying the animals is one way to enjoy wildlife, but recognizing interactions between individuals will enhance your enjoyment. Since animals often come close to each other when feeding, and since food is a very precious commodity, there are bound to be confrontations.

One of the first and most basic rules of interaction at a feeder is that, in almost all cases, the bigger animal has first choice. That is why it's a good idea to have small feeders for small birds and bigger feeders for the larger birds. If both types are provided, then large and small animals can feed at the same time without conflict.

Within a single species of bird that attends a feeding station there is frequently a dominance hierarchy. One individual is top "dog," another is second "dog," another third, and so on down the line. If number one is on the feeder, it will displace any lower ranking bird that comes by. If a lower ranking bird is on the feeder and a higher ranking bird arrives, the lower ranking bird gives way. Black-capped chickadees show a very distinct ranking in their family groups.

When a lower ranking bird is displaced from a feeder it may often fly to a nearby branch and wipe its bill. This is probably not like humans using a napkin after eating. Bill wiping in this situation is actually a displacement activity.

A displacement activity is when you do something other than what you really want to do.   For example, if your boss chews you out, you know you can't read your boss the riot act in defense, so you go home and "kick the dog," yell at your spouse, or beat a ball against the wall. A displaced low ranking bird would like to keep its position on the feeder,   but it can't, so it flies away and wipes its bill as a way of venting its "frustration."

Bill wiping is often a displacement activity, something you do other than what you really want to do.

Starlings in our yard will bill wipe on branches after   their   unsuccessful attempts to evict a downy woodpecker from its excavation. Because a starling cannot excavate its own nest hole, it must confiscate a new hole or an unused hole. When a starling saw the downy woodpecker excavating in a branch of our red maple, it immediately investigated. A starling's large size and aggressive nature would normally be no challenge to a downy woodpecker, but its large size prevented it from using the small hole. In its frustration the starling flew away to a branch and began bill wiping.

Several postures and vocalizations displayed at feeding stations serve as threats to "watch your step." These threats are quite effective, so seldom do animals physically come to blows. But watching their interactions adds to the enjoyment of a feeding station.

The Fine Art Of
Behavior Watching

The natural world is full of discoveries. Its endless variety of species could keep an individual searching for years. In fact, in order to see all the animals on the earth, one would have to see 48 species per day (based on a life span of 75 years). And that does not include plants.

But most people see the same species over and over again, rather than seeing new species each day. In order to keep that thrill of discovery, look for new behaviors of familiar species.

Behavior watching can lead to some interesting discoveries. For instance, one day the staff at the Independence Oaks Nature Center in Michigan watched a gray squirrel eat a female house finch. Yes, a bird. It found the bird dead at the base of the wall by the windows. Probably a window kill.

Then without hesitation, it picked up the bird and carried it to a branch of the nearest tree and proceeded to eat it. Only feathers were left.

Typically we think of squirrels as eating seeds, nuts and an occasional insect. This was indeed atypical behavior, but maybe it happens more frequently than we think. If given an opportunity to supplement their diet, squirrels may take advantage of the situation. Thirteen-lined ground squirrels are a typical seed-eating rodent, but their diet is supplemented with frogs, snakes, birds and mammals.

A gray squirrel with a house finch.

One of the larger birds of prey found in Michigan is the osprey. People fishing the rivers and lakes of northern Michigan see them fly overhead as they look for fish too. Their diet was once thought to be solely fish. But one observer saw a bird walking on the ground chasing after rodents. It must have been very awkward for the bird to run with its long talons designed for catching fish.

There is also an atypical situation that is often mentioned in ornithology books of a cardinal feeding goldfish at a small backyard pond. It is believed the bird's nest had recently been destroyed and it still had the urge to feed something. When it saw the goldfish gaping at the pond the bird was stimulated to feed.

So if anyone ever asks if squirrels only eat seeds, or if osprey only eat fish, or if adult birds only feed their young...

Never say always.

Lifeless But Alive
Dead Trees

During the summer when lush green leaves are on plants, dead trees and their "skeletonized" forms contrast sharply with the full bodied look of leafy trees. To some these are "eyesores" and are often removed. To naturalists and animals, they are an important phase in the life cycle of a tree.

New, healthy trees supply leaves for animals to eat. They provide nuts, fruits and berries which serve as food for many animals, including people. Leafy branches serve as protection from enemies and the elements and they also provide oxygen for all living things.

If a tree should die because of a lack of water or sunlight, fungus infection, wind or lighting damage, a new phase of its importance begins. Wood begins to soften and woodpeckers can excavate a hole to serve as a nesting site. Woodpeckers will also be able to probe and search for insects which have invaded the sickened tree.

Abandoned woodpecker holes are occupied by other hole nesters such as chickadees and titmice. They are dependent on woodpeckers or natural cavities for nesting sites since they cannot excavate holes in hard wood. Another resident of abandoned woodpecker holes are flying squirrels.

By now a wide variety of insects have taken up residence in the tree. Carpenter ants tunnel through the decaying wood, while bark beetles create channels that can be seen as flakes of bark begin to peel away. Honey bees may also build a hive in a natural cavity formed inside the tree.

Mammals seek refuge inside the tree, too. During the cold months of winter, raccoons, squirrels and opossum find warmth and protection in dead tree cavities.

Hawks can often be seen perched on leafless dead branches because it provides them with an unobstructed view. This habit helps hawk watchers spot them.

A tree may be dead, but it is not lifeless. Many plants and animals depend on this later stage of the life cycle of a tree. Even when it falls to the ground, a host of plants and animals depend on its nutrients and shelter. Fungus and moss use the fallen tree for food and as a foundation. Millipedes and salamanders use it as a shelter.

So if you have a "dead" tree that is not causing any concern to property or human health, let it be. It will provide many opportunities to awake to wildlife.

Hawking Flycatchers

One of the nice things about an interest in nature is that no matter where you go there is something you can observe and appreciate. Traveling around the state, or across the states, naturalists find interest in the similarities and differences in the natural world.

For instance, one day I was lying on a table giving blood at our local Red Cross. Fortunately, my table was next to a window, so instead of counting the holes in the ceiling tiles, I could see outside. As I looked at the trees, I noticed some movement that turned out to be a bird. After watching its "hawking" type hunting behavior - searching for prey from a branch, flying to capture the prey, and then returning to the branch - I identified it as a flycatcher. After a few more moments and some changes in positioning so I could see some color, it turned out to be a great-crested flycatcher. I continued squeezing my hand and in no time I was finished.

Flycatchers, as their name implies, feed primarily on insects. Watching their abrupt turns and erratic flight, you can trace the movement of insects. To help them catch insects in flight, flycatchers have wide mouths and long whiskers (rictal bristles) that protrude from the base of their bills. When an insect touches a whisker, the flycatcher is directed to its location and immediately grabs it in its bill.

Shallow, rapid wingbeats aid flycatchers in catching insects, but they also help us to identify them at a distance.

Shallow, rapid wingbeats aid flycatchers in catching insects, but they also help us to identify them at a distance. A partial crest, not as prominent as of a cardinal's, and their habit of returning to the same branch after short feeding flights helps identify flycatchers in general.

Great-crested flycatchers nest in tree cavities. Natural holes or old woodpecker excavations may be used. Birds can also be induced into artificial nest boxes. No matter where the nest is, great-crested flycatchers have the curious habit of lining their nests with a shed snake skin. People have speculated as to why, but no one knows for sure. Some nests have onion skins or cellophane as substitutes for snake skins - maybe shininess is the attraction.

Whether driving down the road, sitting on your front porch, weeding your garden, or giving blood, you can observe the wonders of the natural world.

Bad Apples And Curious Children

Walking with young children can be interesting for all. It is amazing what they can find in ordinary places.

To the eyes of a toddler, everything is new and boredom is unknown. Just walking down the sidewalk precipitates several stops where ants are crawling in the cracks. Being much closer to the ground helps them see things that adults miss. But most of the time, I feel it's their innocent curiosity that directs them.

While my one-and-a-half year-old son and I walked around the block one day, he stopped to investigate a fallen apple the size of a ping-pong ball. Most of it was green, but a portion was brown from decay.

As he picked it up, the movement must have stimulated an ant to exit the apple. It crawled onto his thumb and then back on the apple trying to figure out where the land had gone.

We put that apple down so the ant could find its home, but in the time it takes to blink an eye my son had another one. It was larger but was half eaten. We saw small grooves in the meat of the apple, probably the result of a deer mouse nibbling on it last night.

Investigating this apple reminded me of the many wild apple trees I have seen in meadows and along fence rows. Fruit that had fallen to the ground often showed signs of being eaten by both mice and ants. In rural areas, deer tracks were frequently seen beneath

the tree.

The apple tree in the fence row was probably planted by one of 25 different species of birds that regularly feed on apples. Sometimes the seeds pass through their digestive systems untouched. It's interesting that some seeds must pass through the digestive system of an animal in order to be softened before germination can occur.

In our neighborhood, squirrels, skunks, opossum, rabbits and raccoons may also feast on the fallen fruit. Slugs and bacteria will use the nutrients stored in the apple. And even as the decaying apple disappears into the ground, earthworms will feed on the nutrients absorbed into the soil.

At the time, my son was only interested in something new along the sidewalk, but if it were not for his stopping to investigate I would not have been aware of any animal eating those apples. Adults need more of that innocent curiosity that toddlers have in abundance.

Ilia Underwing Moth

Becoming a wildlife watcher and alerting others to this wonderful recreation can be very gratifying. The pleasure of an initial experience is doubled when it is shared with someone else who is interested. Over time friends and acquaintances will share many stories and learn from each other.

People frequently bring natural subjects to me for identification. This shows me the person has an interest in the diversity of life. An awareness, coupled with some information about the plant or animal, can often lead to an appreciation of it.

I personally enjoy the challenge of helping people identify something. It is much easier to identify the subject in its natural habitat than from a verbal description but there are times I can't even name something in my hand. The natural world is so diverse that nobody can identify everything.

One day a friend found a large caterpillar near his home. He brought it to work, hoping I could identify it for him.

I couldn't, but I was interested to see the two-inch-long larva with a lavender belly and mottled brown back. From above, it was camouflaged, but when it was turned onto its back, exposing the lavender belly, it immediately flipped onto its belly. Even more amazing was the response time of this flipping - within the blink of an eye.

We put the larva in a jar with some soil and a small branch with leaves. Some caterpillars develop a cocoon on tree branches, while some develop a pupal case underground.

Within a couple days, the larva enclosed itself in a pupal case underground. A month later, it emerged as a beautiful Ilia underwing moth.

It had a large body, about the size of my little finger, underwings with orange-pink and black stripes, and upperwings that were colored like the bark of a tree.

After we had a chance to observe the adult, we let it loose outside so it could continue the cycle of life. Within a short time, the adult moth would mate and die. Most moths do not overwinter as adults.

Sharing like this is a learning experience for all involved and is a non-destructive way of enjoying the outdoors. Perpetuating this kind of attitude, in both adults and children, can lead people to a more harmonious association with nature.

Navigation, Constellations And Bird Migration

All the migrant birds that breed in the Great Lakes area have returned from their wintering grounds by early June. Some species, such as cardinals, chickadees, and nuthatches, remain here all winter and begin nesting early in the season. Others, such as northern orioles, scarlet tanagers and house wrens return from wintering grounds in places such as Central America, Peru, and Texas.

They generally fly north during the night at about 40 miles per hour. Depending on the weather conditions, they fly at an elevation of about 4,000 feet. On clear nights birds fly higher than on cloudy overcast nights.

During the day, they rest, feed, and wait for favorable weather conditions before continuing their journeys. Their flights north in spring are usually rushed because it is to their advantage to get to the breeding area as soon as possible. Males want to get first choice of the best breeding territories.

It has been determined from banding studies that most birds return to the area where they were raised. So the wren that has been nesting in your backyard for the last couple of years is likely to be the same wren. Young raised by those adults will return to the same general area to raise their young.

Even before we learned that individual birds return to the same area year after year, man has been intrigued by the phenomenon of bird migration. How do the birds find their way from South America all the way to your backyard?

MIGRATING birds ARE able TO NAVIGATE by usiNG coNSTEllatioNS aNd TO COMPENSATE for their rotatioN arouNd the North Star.

That mystery has not been solved, but we do know some of the methods they use to orient themselves. Migrating birds are able to navigate by using constellations and to compensate for their rotation around the North Star. They also use the sun and adjust for its movement across the sky. Pigeons are able to detect the Earth's magnetic field and use it in orientation. There may even be other mechanisms that we have not discovered yet.

When you see your backyard migrants return each year, you can marvel at their ability to travel such distances and to return to the same area year after year.

Dustbowls & Bird Baths

Summer is indeed the time for bathing. On hot sticky days, or after one has been sun bathing, it feels great to cool off in the shower. Well, man is not the only animal that bathes. We are all familiar with birds splashing in a shallow puddle formed by the sprinkler. Wetting feathers with water can help control their body heat, help align their feathers and control parasites.

Birds do not always use water to bathe with either. Ants, believe it or not, are used in bathing by birds. Several species of birds have been seen lying on an ant mound and intentionally allowing ants to crawl all over their bodies. It is believed that ants help control parasites by leaving behind traces of formic acid which they produce.

Birds also sun bathe. On hot sunny days one may see a robin or cardinal in the yard resting on the ground with its wings outstretched and head arched downward. It may appear that the bird is suffering from heat exhaustion, but it is actually sun bathing.

Sun bathing is believed to force ectoparasites to regions of the body where the bird can easily remove them. Exposing the skin to sunlight may stimulate the production of vitamin D. There is also a strong correlation between molting and sun bathing. Sunlight may help to soothe skin irritated by the replacement of new feathers.

Several species of birds have been reported bathing in the rain and in the dew on leaves. But dust bathing is not as common. Fowl like birds, such as quail, pheasants and grouse, are those most

A bird taking a dust bath.

commonly observed dust bathing.

One day I had the opportunity to watch a ruffed grouse dust bathing. Like most birds that dust bathe, this individual rocked back and forth to form a slight depression in an old ant mound. It was very deliberate in its movements and would lie on one side for a short period of time with the upper wing extended. This allowed dust to get into the underwing area.

There were times when it rolled onto its back while rocking and rolling to and fro insuring dust landed everywhere. In between bouts of rocking it would remain still for long periods as if soaking in pleasure. Though this behavior made the bird more vulnerable to predation, it stayed in its "tub" for about 40 minutes.

The exact function of dust bathing is not known, but it is thought to remove excess lipids from the feathers which are fed upon by feather mites. It may also help fluff the feathers and aid in their alignment.

Summer Birdfeeding

Feeding birds during winter has become a popular source of entertainment in recent years. Many people enjoy seeing the red-colored cardinal come for a snack of sunflower seed, or the American goldfinch nibbling on a thistle seed.

Providing a nutritious source of food for birds during the winter, when food is scarce, serves both birds and birder. But some people have asked me, "Do I need to feed birds during the summer, too?"

The direct answer is no. Birds can find sufficient food during summer when insects and other food sources abound. Actually, studies indicate that birds derive about 20 percent of their food from feeders. Remember, birds have been around the Great Lakes for 14,000 years before bird feeders became established. During that time they did quite well without our help.

Winter is a hard time for animals like birds, especially during a two- or three-day storm. Staying warm takes a lot of energy. If an animal cannot get sufficient food it will perish. Bird feeders supply that readily available source of food during storms when natural food is hard to find.

Late spring is also a critical time of the year for birds. Most of the winter food supply has been used, yet cold temperatures and sudden storms may occur, and the rigors of establishing a territory or laying eggs result in increased energy demands.

Though conditions are much more favorable in summer, there

are reasons why you may want to consider feeding birds in summer. First of all, even seed-eating birds like cardinals feed their young nestlings insects. Insects provide a more nutritious source of food for growing bodies than seeds. So if you provide a constant source of food for the adults, you free up their time to search out hard-to-find insects for their young. Even if the adults just supplement their own diet, it will still save them time.

The second advantage is that you can see the young birds as they come to the feeder. One day my wife and I watched a mother downy woodpecker and her young at our suet feeder. As the adult probed into the suet, it picked out small bits and fed them to the young on the side of the feeder. After awhile she would not give suet to the young bird despite its begging intentions. This was undoubtedly a way to coax the young into feeding for itself.

A few days later, we saw dad feeding his son, who had by then learned how to feed on his own quite well - but he never missed a free handout from dad when it was offered.

If you provide a source of food for the adults during the summer, you free up their time to search out hard-to-find insects for their young.

In this way, the youngster learns that suet is good to eat. He also learns how to eat it and he knows where to find it. *Eat at the Nowicki's! They have sweet suet and scrumptious seeds!*

Any way of increasing your opportunities to view wildlife and to observe their unique ways is worth considering.

Playful Young Squirrels

When my wife and I were expecting our first child, we prepared for the baby's arrival by reading books and articles on child development. We also started making the house ready for a young child by covering electrical outlets and putting breakable items up high.

Our anticipation made me more aware of the young living things around me - from the maple and elm seeds helicoptering to the ground, to the continued growth and development of the young squirrels in the backyard.

We had quite a collection of squirrels in our yard in those days. They provided us free entertainment throughout the year. In January they would run up and down and around the trees, one closely following the other, like the stripe on a moving barber's sign. That activity was part of courtship.

Nest building was easy to identify. Our yard was full of small twigs and leaves that would later be carried up the tree to build the nest. Near the end of June we watched as the mother squirrel began the weaning process by refusing to let the youngster climb on her back or to follow her to the nest. That process certainly comes sooner in a squirrel's life than in a human's.

The young squirrel accepted the change very well, though. Many times we saw it tumbling and rollicking on the lawn with sticks and clods of dirt, like a kitten with a ball of yarn.

At times they would jump straight up into the air from a standing position, twist 180 degrees in the air, land and then race

up the nearest tree for no apparent reason.

Play behavior like this helps to develop the animal's coordination and perception. It also develops its rank and position in the squirrel community when it interacts with other squirrels.

Play, as most parents know, can result in accidents and hard knocks. One morning I saw a young squirrel fall 30 feet to the ground from the branches of our oak tree. It quickly climbed a few feet up the tree trunk, but then came down to the ground and remained motionless.

After 10 minutes of staring at the ground in front of it, the animal slowly wandered off. Soon after that we saw it tussling with others, so everything ended up alright. But I am sure that it learned not to make the same mistake that led to its 30-foot fall.

Plastic, Cellophane, Fiberglas
Man-made Bird Nests

For thousands of years, birds have been building their nests of natural material. A typical songbird builds the foundation of its nest out of coarse twigs, grasses, shreds of bark or mud. It lines the cup of the nest, where the young are found, with fine, soft materials such as mosses, animal hair, or seed silk from thistle or willow.

Man, too, once used only natural material for construction. But now plows are made of steel, chairs from plastic and clothes from nylon - all synthetic materials. Birds typically use natural material, but they are not beyond using some man-made products.

While trimming our hedge one day I found an abandoned nest tucked in the branches. Finding the nest was not surprising, but identifying the material used was. Woven in the foundation of the nest was the plastic retainer that holds six cans of pop together. There was a notched plastic tie-wrap and some plastic banding material.

Not long after that I cleaned out a house sparrow nest from our attic and discovered numerous cellophane wrappers in the nest. Though there was a great deal of man-made material, it still had a large amount of grasses.

Many years ago I remember a nest made exclusively of synthetic material. A northern oriole nest found near the Fred Bear Archery Museum and factory in Grayling, Michigan was made entirely of fiberglass. The adult birds took Fiberglas shavings from the factory and used them to make their nest. Though the nest must have been extremely durable, imagine how itchy those naked nestlings must have been! It reminds me of when my underwear got washed with some fiberglass curtains. I definitely had an itchy sensation.

Looking for nests when the leaves have fallen from the trees and bushes can be very enlightening. Most nests remain undetected until the cloak of leaves is removed. Then, not only is the nest discovered, but you may find some interesting adaptations to the world of manmade objects as well.

Though it may seem harmless to collect abandoned nests, it is against the law. Remember the old saying: *Take only pictures, leave only footprints.*

Tools Of Survival

While walking along a trail in a Detroit area park one day, I heard a sound that I could not positively identify - short bursts of sound which were very penetrating and quite loud.

It was the intensity of the sound that perplexed me. The sound was so loud that I anticipated seeing the animal right around the next tree. Yet, it was even too loud for that situation.

I do not remember how far away from the source I actually started hearing the sound, but it was much farther than I would have heard a normal chipmunk calling. Yes, my mystery caller was

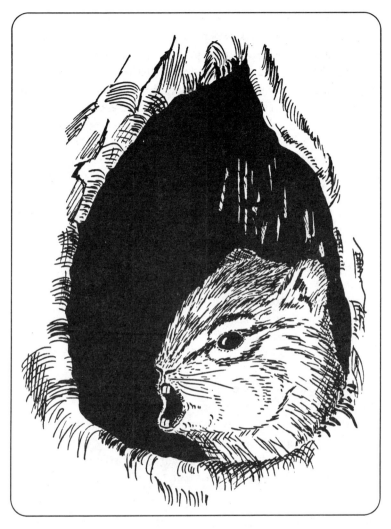

a chipmunk, whose sound I have heard often, but not like this one.

This chipmunk was in the hollow of a large tree which opened in the direction from which I had been walking. There, perched in the opening near the bottom was the resounding vocalizer. The hollow cavity served as a reflector and resonating chamber, which amplified the sound.

Chipmunks call to warn others of danger and to establish territories. This individual apparently discovered that the hollow of a tree intensifies the sound, which could help in communicating to others. By using the tree hollow, this individual sounded like a 200-pound chipmunk calling to warn others to stay away from its territory.

Though I did not return to see if the animal used this location regularly, or to see if it used other hollows, this animal could be defined as a tool user. It was using an object to help it perform a necessary function.

This animal could be defined as a tool user. It was using an object to help it perform a necessary function.

Actually, tool using in animals is not that extremely rare. Every day I watch woodpeckers take sunflower seeds and wedge them in the crack of a wooden pole. They hammer at the seed to break open the husk and extract the kernel. Behavior like this reminds me of when I use the vice on my bench.

Herring gulls have been observed dropping clams and snails on hard objects in order to break open the hard shells. They did not use just any hard object; they repeatedly returned to one specific place.

Animals have both physical and behavioral adaptations to their changing environment.

Hunting Earthworms With
Wood Turtles

When we think of turtles we think of rivers, lakes and ponds. Wetland areas are where we find most turtles found in the Great Lakes region.

But, as with many things, there are exceptions to this rule. Box turtles are truly terrestrial and wood turtles spend a great deal of their time in summer out of water. They can frequently be seen basking in the sun in open fields far from water.

Of the nine native species of turtle found in Michigan, wood turtles have one of the most distinctive shells. In fact, the name wood turtle comes from the similarity between the ringed sculpturing of the upper shell plates, to the concentric rings of a tree trunk. Like the rings of a tree trunk revealing the age of a tree, the rings on the scutes of a wood turtle can indicate the age of a turtle to about 20 years old. Some may argue the name refers to its woodland habitat, but no matter which description you prefer, they are both true.

While traversing woodlands, wood turtles eat a variety of items. Their menu consists of insects, various plant leaves, fruits and mushrooms, but they are particularly fond of earthworms.

This fondness for earthworms has led to a very interesting behavior which is reminiscent of professional worm grunters. Men grunt for worms by rubbing a notched stick or coil spring across a stake which has been driven into the ground. Vibrations created force the worms to the surface and away from the disturbance.

Every year Florida has a national worm grunting championship to see who can collect the most worms in a given time period.

Wood turtles are more subtle in their methods, but just as effective. They gently, but firmly, stomp their feet on the ground. First stomping with their right foot for a while, and then with their left. A researcher imitated this same action with his fingers and was able to force earthworms to the surface.

This fondness for earthworms has led to a very interesting behavior which is reminiscent of professional worm grunters.

Researchers have also experimented with a wood turtle's ability to run a typical maze. Food was placed at the end of tunnels which had three or four right and left turn choices. Their results indicated that the wood turtle mastered the maze as readily as a rat would under the same experimental conditions.

Next time you walk along wetlands or fields in northern Michigan, look on the ground for the unexpected wood turtle; maybe you will catch it grunting for worms.

Bluegills, Snakes & Snappers
Dangerous Nesting

Throughout the years animals and plants have come to rely on things that are consistent. Sunlight is always available and is used to activate the production of food in plants.

As the seasons progress daylight duration varies consistently. Animals and plants have modified their behavior to accommodate these expected changes.

So as the sunlight begins to warm the earth and the daylight period lengthens, animals begin their season of reproduction. Because it is a time to replenish losses, nest sites are carefully selected. Birds choose a nest site so that it is well hidden. Squirrels build a nest high in the trees far from most predators. Burrowing animals keep their young underground, which makes them safe from many predators.

Though nest sites are carefully selected, adults are committed to returning to the site to care for the young. This fact is well known by predators. They intentionally hunt areas with a high concentration of nests or young. If they cannot catch the adult, they will take young instead.

In late spring one year I saw this process verified. Along the shore of Crooked Lake in Michigan, small bluegills were defending shallow depressions they made which serve as nests. Males defend them from other males and at the same time try to attract a female to their nest. When one male gets too close to another's nest, it is chased away. Chases cause disturbances in other surrounding nests, which results in several males scattering in all directions.

In one bed of 10 nests was a northern watersnake lying under water waiting for the fish to return to their nests. Though the fish knew the snake was there, they still returned - cautiously. Some of the fish would hover right in front of the snake's head. But the only time the snake tried to catch a fish was when they scattered for one reason or another. I witnessed several strikes in which the snake never caught a fish.

Then later that same day, in the same lake, only in deeper water, I saw three bluegill nests that were larger. The owners were hovering below the surface but not next to the beds because in between the three beds was a large snapping turtle, taking advantage of the fish as the northern water snake had been.

This kind of hunting technique must be successful or else it would not be evident in two different species.

Wild Iridescence

One of the most striking and fascinating features of the natural world is the diversity of color and patterns. Spring warblers have some very impressive colors and patterns. So do the variety of butterflies that can be seen in summer.

Colors in nature result from either pigments or from the physical structure of a body part. Pigments such as melanin produce the blacks and browns we see in animals. Chlorophyll is the pigment which makes plants green.

Small inchworms, often seen dangling from overhead branches, get their green coloration from eating the leaves of plants. But the green of a hummingbird is produced by the structure of the feathers themselves.

The ultimate in coloration of animals is iridescence. It occurs when sunlight hits small striations in the structure of a feather or the shell of an insect. When sunlight hits the throat of a ruby-throated humming-bird it may look fiery orange or ruby red. If the sun is not shinning on those feathers, they look black.

Birds, like grackles and hummingbirds, are not the only animals which exhibit iridescence. Insects display iridescence in several species. While walking the trails one day I came upon a divergent metallic wood boring beetle.

THE ULTIMATE IN COLORATION OF ANIMALS IS IRI-DESCENCE, CAUSED by SMALL STRIATIONS IN fEATHERS OR THE shELL OF AN INSECT.

This beetle was about three-eights of an inch wide and one and a quarter inches long. From above it did not look very interesting, but when I flipped it over onto its back a shiny copper metallic coloration was revealed.

In more open areas where dogbane and milkweed grow, one can find the dogbane beetle. On a bright sunny day this inch long rounded beetle is a rainbow of colors. As the sunlight is diffracted by as many as 1,400 small striations per millimeter, it is reflected back to our eye as green, blue, red, and yellow. Half of the hard rounded shell not in the sunlight appears black.

Tortoise beetles and some butterflies exhibit a spectacular iridescence also. In order to observe this though, one has to look closely for some of the often unseen natural features.

Sphinx, Hawk And Hummingbirds
Daytime Moths

When comparisons of the natural world and man's artificial world are made, similarities between the systems are remarkable.

Man lives in many different types of settings such as rural, suburban and urban, while animals live in habitats like mountains, forests and meadows. Humans generally have work shifts that are either day, afternoon or night. Among animals, raccoons are active during the night, crepuscular bats in the evening, dirunal fox squirrels during the day.

Like humans that take over the job from the previous shift of workers, animals have shift replacements also. Hawks, for instance, are active during the day but are relieved by owls at night. Butterflies sip nectar during the day, while moths search for nectar at night.

As in any system, there are exceptions. Some owls, like hawk owls and snowy owls, hunt by day, just as some moths probe flowers during the day.

Sphinx, hawk and hummingbird are all common names for one interesting group of moths that can be seen during the day. Among the common names used, sphinx is derived from the defensive reaction of its larva. When a larva is alarmed it arches into a position that resembles an Egyptian sphinx.

Hawk is used as a common name to describe this group of moths because they fly rapidly like hawks. Hummingbird is an appropriate name because the moth resembles a hummingbird in a couple ways.

Both have long narrow wings and an enlarged, elongated body and both hover at flowers during the day. While hovering, the moth may move the tip of its abdomen as the hummingbird moves its tail.

Hiking in meadows full of summer flowers is a place where the observant can see these nectar sippers. It was a sunny day in August when I saw a hummingbird moth enjoying an afternoon mint julep. After stopping in my tracks so I would not disturb it, I realized that it was sipping nectar from the flowers of bergamot, a member of the mint family.

In some species of hummingbird moths, the proboscis (the tubular organ used for sucking food) is twice as long as its body. This allows them to extract nectar from deep-throated flowers like honeysuckle.

Sphinx/hawk/hummingbird moths are the mature adults to the tomato, or tobacco hornworms, or caterpillars, which many gardeners find among their plants. The caterpillars have a harmless horn that protrudes from the rear of the larva.

Its common name is derived from the defensive reaction of its larva. When alarmed it arches into a position that resembles an Egyptian sphinx.

When mature, the larva falls to the ground and develops into a pupa with a "handle." The pupa is brown with a loop at one end which houses the long, developing proboscis.

So the next time you think you see a hummingbird at a flower, take a closer look. It could be a moth.

Rigid, Soft Or Hinged?
The (Turtle) Shell Game

"Theme and variation" is a technique that composers use to write music. A basic melody is modified in many ways. Different instruments may be used, the tempo might be changed, or certain phrases may be lengthened or shortened. No matter how the music is changed, one can still recognize it as a variation of the original theme.

Nature, too, has composed innumerable variations and is an expert at this technique. For instance, everyone can recognize turtles. They all have the same basic shape. All turtles have four legs, a tail and of course a shell. A turtle's upper shell is actually an extension of the backbone (vertebrae) and ribs.

An outer layer of horny material, similar to fingernail, covers the bones of both the upper and lower shells. Periodically, these horny scales are shed and replaced.

Turtles can extend their scaly feet, legs and head when swimming or feeding. But when danger threatens, they retract those soft parts into the hard shell. This method of protection has been used for more than 200 million years.

Most turtle shells are rigid, allowing exposure of the retracted legs. Box turtles, however, have a hinge on the lower shell that allows the animal to completely enclose its body parts. Michigan's "smiling" yellow throated Blanding's turtle also has a hinged lower shell but cannot enclose its body as completely as the box turtle.

Though the lower shell on most turtles is solid, the musk turtle, or stinkpot, has skin that separates the bones. A structure like this is not as protective as a solid, or a hinged shell. Snapping turtles have a small, relatively unprotective lower shell too. Those turtles with little protection from the lower shell stay in the water most of the time and also have a pugnacious attitude. Both of these behavioral characteristics help to protect the turtle when its shell will not.

A further variation is an entirely soft shell. One species of turtle in the Great Lakes area has a pliable or leathery shell. It is called the soft-shelled turtle. They have a long nose and neck which can be extended to capture food or to gather air while buried in a stream bed.

Some turtle shells look smooth and plain, in contrast to the individual scales of the wood turtle which look like the growth rings of a tree. Painted turtles have colorful borders to their shells, and the spotted turtle naturally has spots.

Color, shape, texture, pattern, structure and size are a few of the variations that are exhibited on the theme of a turtle.

BOX TURTLES HAVE A HINGE ON THE LOWER SHELL THAT ALLOWS THE ANIMAL TO COMPLETELY ENCLOSE ITS BODY PARTS.

A northern oriole.

Color In The Sun

When watching wildlife in the field, or in a backyard, it is important to have the sun at your back. Sunlight is necessary to bring out the color of an animal so we can enjoy its true beauty. Feathers look much better in sunlight, as well as fur and the exoskeleton of insects.

One morning I gathered with a group in a parking lot in preparation for a morning of birdwatching. While we were getting ready and practicing with our binoculars, someone spotted a northern oriole (formerly the Baltimore oriole). As we watched the bird for a while, we discovered its nest in a sycamore tree.

In a short time, we saw both adults near the nest. The male was near the top of the tree in the sunlight, while the female was in the shadows, bringing food to the nestlings. When the male was perched in the open and exposed to the direct sunlight, his orange body feathers appeared so bright they almost looked artificial. Direct sunlight allows pigment and feather structure to work together to create the most intense color.

As we walked along the trail, we found another bird that demonstrated this principle. An indigo bunting, a small finch, was spotted in some low bushes near the trail. Looking at the bird in the shadows did not reveal why this species is called "indigo." But as soon as the male was exposed to sunlight, the rich, royal blue color of his feathers became evident.

Though most mammals do not perceive color the way man does, birds have excellent color perception. Some of the most colorful living creatures are birds or animals that birds eat.

Many insects are boldly colored to alert birds and other predators to stay away because they are distasteful. These bold patterns and brilliant colors are easily remembered by a bird after it encounters a noxious insect.

In addition to observing several species of birds, we saw a number of white-tailed deer. Two young bucks with their early antler growth in thick velvet ran across an open field right in front of us. Their reddish summer coats glowed in the sunlight just like the feathers of the birds we saw.

In order to see and appreciate the variety and patterns of color in wildlife, it is best to see them in open sunlight. Our last example of this phenomenon was the male eastern bluebird we saw by its nest box. Only when he flew into the open did we see the blue that makes him so attractive.

JUST WHAT IS GUANO?

Guano is the scientific community's word for bird droppings. It may not sound like a very interesting topic, but its significance came to light with some experiences I had.

If the topic of guano ever came up during the course of conversation, it was probably because it landed on a recently washed car or laundry hanging on the line to dry.

There are times when I speculate as to why birds sit on wires crossing over busy roads. I imagine them discussing how many shiny new cars they had hit today, and if any of them really scored a bull's-eye by hitting the driver's side window. Maybe I have been reading too many Far Side cartoons.

Well, enough of the negative side of guano. There is a positive side. Guano has a very high concentration of nitrogen. On some South American islands where sea birds have nested for centuries, guano has accumulated to depths of 165 feet. Companies mined the guano for fertilizers because of its high nitrogen content.

Birds actually produce uric acid rather than urea as mammals do. Before waste leaves the body, most of the water is reabsorbed, producing the concentrated uric acid. This water saving adapation allows many birds to surrive on water found only in their food. Excrement of birds is a combination of liquid and solid waste. That is why it tends to be very pasty.

If the topic of guano ever comes up, it's probably because it landed on a recently washed car.

One summer, I watched a viceroy butterfly caterpillar form a chrysalis. As the caterpillar made its transformation, the resulting chrysalis took on the shape and color of a bird dropping clinging to a branch. I also got a chance to watch a red-spotted purple emerge from a chrysalis that resembled a bird dropping. Both butterfly species are closely related, which is why the chrysalis of each is remarkably similar.

Very young swallowtail caterpillars resemble a fresh bird dropping. Then later, after they have grown larger, they develop eye spots that are designed to scare away potential predators.

As I walk along trails in the Great Lakes area I have noticed many white-colored moths lying exposed with their wings outspread on green leaves. At first it seems that this behavior would expose them to predators. However, a quick glance to some real whitewash or guano on a nearby leaf will clarify the reason for this behavior. Both moth and guano look similar, and since no self-respecting animal is going to eat guano, the moth and chrysalis are safe.

Now Introducing The HOUSE FINCH

At a small family gathering in 1986, I identified a male house finch singing on a wire. Twenty years ago this bird was unknown in the Midwest. House finches arrived in southeastern Michigan in recognizable numbers during the late 1970s and early 1980s.

Those birds that moved into the midwestern states are part of a population of birds that started in New York City about fifty years ago. In 1940, California cage-bird dealers sent shipments of house finches to New York to be sold as "California Finches." (Before they were transplanted their range was restricted to west of the Rockies.) Authorities learned of this illegal transaction and were in the process of confiscating birds, but several dealers just released their birds instead of being fined. By 1943 many of those released birds were nesting in the New York City area.

Since their release in New York City house finches have been expanding westward. House finches have adapted well to urban environments and the midwestern climate. They nest in a variety of places - tree cavities, low shrubs, tin cans and even old swallow nests. My aunt had one nesting under her awning and many people report them nesting in wreaths on doors.

Ellie Cox of the Oakland Audubon Society has been documenting their dispersal in the metropolitan Detroit area. She documented nesting for downtown Detroit in 1982. By 1986 they were in several suburban areas. According to *The Atlas of Breeding Birds of Michigan*, published in 1991, their nesting expanded as far north as Rogers City, Michigan.

House finches are the size of house sparrows, which were, incidentally, also introduced into New York in 1850. Male house finches have bright red on their crowns and upper parts; their backs are brown; the sides of their bellies are streaked. Females are brown and heavily streaked.

Songs of house finches are pleasant, high-pitched warbles, much more interesting than the chirp of the house sparrow. They are attracted to a variety of seeds and food sources, both in summer and winter.

Since their release house finches have been expanding westward and have adapted well to urban environments.

For summer residents of Michigan in the southern three tiers of counties, most red headed "sparrows" at feeders are likely to be house finches. Those residents in the middle part of the state may also have the kissing cousin of the house finch, the purple finch, at their feeders. Male purple finch have a different shade of red on the head and upper breast compared to the house finch, and they do not have prominent streaking on the sides. Some naturalists compare the red of a purple finch with raspberries and the red of the house finch with strawberries. This difference is noticeable when the two species are together, but it's difficult for beginners to distinguish between the two when they are seen separately. Female purple finches have a definite white line above the eye and a whiter breast contrasting with the brown of the back.

During winter purple finch can move into the southern part of the Great Lakes and allow feeder watchers to enjoy both species.

Checks And Balances
Caterpillars & Cuckoos

All living things overproduce because only a small fraction of young will ever reach adulthood. Checks and balances have been incorporated into man's world, but not nearly to the extent that they are found in nature because most organisms serve as food for others at various stages in their lives.

In 1988, many people commented to me that there seemed to be an unusually large number of tent caterpillars in our area. These are the caterpillars that build a white, spider web-looking tent in the crotch of a black cherry tree in early spring.

Young caterpillars hatch from a dark-colored, hard, foam-looking egg mass laid last year at the end of a branch by a female. Upon hatching, young caterpillars make their way to the main trunk of the tree and begin to build their spider web-like shelter. During the day they feed on young leaves at the end of branches. At dusk they return to the shelter of the tent to spend the night.

When they leave the tent they lay down a silken trail laden with a chemical that will guide them back to the tent, since they do not have branch signs to direct them. They even have a special chemical that is laid down when one caterpillar finds a rich food supply and returns to the tent to alert others of its discovery.

As they grow, they enlarge their tent, which also becomes dirty. In order to grow, they must shed their skin. Shedding is done

A cuckoo at a caterpillar tent.

in the security of the tent and those remnant skins collect inside the tent. By the time they are about ready to leave their tent, it looks pretty spotty.

Once a caterpillar matures, it forms a cocoon and will develop into a moth. Like many animals, their populations fluctuate in cycles.

During peaks in their population cycle, large numbers of caterpillars on a small tree can defoliate it, stressing the tree by forcing it to produce another set of leaves. But as their numbers increase in an area, they also attract a bird that feeds on them. Yellow-billed and black-billed cuckoos tend to appear where there are outbreaks of tent caterpillars.

There are always some cuckoos around, but there seem to be

more in years when there is a high population of tent caterpillars. Not many birds eat tent caterpillars, so if you investigate a tent with large holes piercing the exterior, they were probably made by the probing bill of the cuckoo. I've noticed some tents have been totally eradicated by foraging cuckoos.

Unlike their European relative for which cuckoo clocks were named, our cuckoos are not parasitic - they do not lay their eggs in the nests of other birds.

They are long and slender with either a black or a mostly yellow bill. Their upper parts are a medium gray-brown color extending into long tails. Underneath, they are white from chin to belly, but their tails are only spotted with white.

One does not often see them fly because of their secretive nature. But if you do get a look at one, notice the siena color in their open wings. If you ever find one dead, as I did on the side of a road, note the beautiful colors in the wings and look at their feet. Unlike most of our perching birds that have three toes forward and one backward, cuckoos have two toes forward and two toes backward - similar to a woodpecker.

Populations of most organisms fluctuate within limits because of the checks and balances that nature has built in.

Cuckoos tend to appear whenever there are major outbreaks of tent caterpillars.

Bird Watching? How About...
Fish Watching

Fish watching may not be as popular as bird watching or fishing for that matter, but it can be a very interesting pastime. Those with tropical fish at home are fish watchers. Scuba divers and people who snorkel over coral reefs do so mainly to see the multitude of colorful fish below the plain of the ocean's surface.

Michigan does not harbor colorful fish such as those of a coral reef, but some of the sunfish found in our area, like the common bluegill, have interesting patterns and colors. Bluegill vary in color depending on the surroundings of the lake. Colors may range from yellow to blue to almost colorless.

Bluegills have a large black spot on the gill covers that does not have a border. Though most species of sunfish have the flattened shape of the bluegill, the borderless black spot helps to distinguish it from other species.

Shallow water near the edge of ponds or lakes often allows bluegill viewing. When the water temperature reaches about 67 degrees, males begin developing a nest. A male bluegill will fan a sandy area, about 8 inches in diameter, with his tail to expose the stones and pebbles below.

While excavating the nest, he is also trying to attract a female and will defend it from intruding males. The male swims back and forth around the nest exposing his colors in an effort to lure a female to deposit as many as 38,000 eggs in the nest.

After fertilization by the male, eggs will hatch in two to five days.

Young are protected by the male for a few days, but then they are on their own. In the Great Lakes region, young grow about one inch every year, if they survive. A three-year-old bluegill will be four to six inches long.

As you watch nest building, courtship, and territorial defense in the shallows of a pond, you may also see them feed on insects. Mayflies and damselflies are favorite foods, along with small crustaceans.

It is sometimes hard to remember that there is as much variety of life under water as there is on land. Because we do not see aquatic life very much, we tend to forget about its activities. Visit some local ponds and lakes soon and do a little fish watching.

Nature's World Of Doubles
Who's Who???

I do not know if it is true or not, but I have always heard that every person has a double, or someone that looks like him or her somewhere in the world. If you consider the number of people in the world and the number of facial characteristics that can vary, chances are we do have a double.

Casual observations of plants will also reveal "doubles". Many different kinds of plants look similar because they are very closely related. Those who think there is only one species of goldenrod should look more closely. There are some plants, like ash and walnut, which have similar looking leaves but are not related.

Look-alikes are often found in the animal world too. A classic example known by many people is the similarity of the viceroy and monarch butterflies. Orange and black coloration of the monarch warns potential predators that it is distasteful. These bold colors help predators to re-member that they are not suitable for eating.

Viceroy butterflies do not eat milkweed, which is what makes the monarch taste bad, and thus were thought for many years to be palatable to predators. Because their coloration is so similar to the monarch, the viceroy was thought to be protected from predators that had encountered a distasteful monarch. New experiments, however, indicate that the viceroy is just as distasteful as the mon-arch. No matter what situation exists, their similar coloration warns predators and protects both species.

Monarch and viceroy butter-flies are similar in their colora-tion and their foul taste to predators who mistakenly eat them.

Similar colors and patterns can be seen in five species of snake found in Michigan. Northern watersnakes, eastern hognose, massasauga, milk and fox snake can be easily confused. In this complex of ani-mals, it is the habitat and habits of the animals which make this pattern the most effective for survival.

Unfortunately for the snakes that look like Michigan's only poisonous snake, the massasauga, they are often persecuted as the poisonous type.

Moths can even look like hummingbirds or bumble-bees. Sphinx moths often feed during the day and are about the size of hummingbirds. A casual glance could easily mistake a moth for a bird.

Smaller moths with clear wings like a bumblebee, and with yellow and black coloration in the same pattern as a bumblebee, resemble this stinging insect as a means of protection.

In The Shade Of
The Apple Tree

When I was a young man, my grandfather and I spent hours talking, dreaming and relaxing under an apple tree in his front yard. Its shade in summer was very cooling, but its pleasant fragrance and constant hum of honey bees in spring, when the flowers were blooming, made it a special place to whittle away the hours.

One noticeable distinguishing feature of the tree that has remained visible through the years are pock marks formed by a yellow-bellied sapsucker. All around the main trunk and several main branches of the tree are small half-inch long and a quarter-inch wide rectangular holes in the bark. Sapsuckers excavate these holes and feed on the sap that fills the holes. They will also eat any insects that are attracted to the sap wells.

Though the trunk was scarred, the apple tree continued to produce not only apples, but also birds. For as long as I can remember, there has always been at least one species of bird nesting in the tree during the summer.

One species, the eastern kingbird, was probably the most regular nesting species found in the tree. Kingbirds are very aggressive in protecting their nest and young and will ward off other kingbirds, as well as other birds that come near. Kingbirds have also been known to attack cats that venture too close to their nests.

In 1986, however, three species nested in the tree at the same time. A family of kingbirds was at the western edge. Common grackles were nesting on the northern edge, and a rose-breasted grosbeak raised a brood on the eastern edge.

As we sat in the shade of the apple tree that year and relaxed in the glow of the setting sun, we watched a female grosbeak feed her young fledgling insects she had caught. At the other end of the tree, the kingbird regularly scolded the grackle when she came to feed her young in the nest.

Each species of bird tolerated the presence of a different species of bird in the same tree, but they would not tolerate another pair of the same species nesting in the same tree. Some species, like grackles, nest in loose colonies where pairs nest closer than non-colonial nesting species. Most birds, like the kingbird and the grosbeak, will not allow another pair to nest within their established territories.

In years past, we would put short strands of string on the ground under the tree and watch cedar waxwings fly down, pick them up, take them back to the nest, and weave them among the natural materials.

Patiently observing an area, or a subject, over a period of years can be very rewarding, especially if it is as productive as my grandfather's apple tree.

Counting With Katydids

Anyone who falls asleep with the window open on a warm September evening knows that crickets and katydids are busy calling to potential mates. High in the trees, katydids - less than three inches long - produce a noise that makes it sound a foot or longer.

Katydids produce a sound that mimics the cadence of the name katydid. This sound is produced by a file-like structure at the base of the wing cover, which is then rubbed by a scraper, a thickened area at the edge of the other wing. The scraper is developed only on the left side, so all katydids are left-handed singers. Certain crickets are only right-handed singers.

Each species of cricket or katydid produces a song of a certain pitch and a unique cadence. Females are attracted only to the call of their own species.

The frequency of calls is dependent on temperature. In fact, a researcher worked out formulas so one can calculate the temperature by knowing the number of chirps per minute. To test the formula, I counted the number of times a katydid sang in our yard for five minutes. I took the average number of chirps - 50 per minute - and plugged it into the formula.

A RESEARCHER ONCE COUNTED A TREE CRICKET WHICH CHIRPED 2,640 TIMES WITHOUT STOPPING.

Subtract 19 from 50, divide the remainder (31) by 3, and then add 60 to the quotient - and you can determine the temperature in Fahrenheit. I calculated 70. Our radio station weather forecaster reported a temperature of 72.

Its important to use the correct formula because substituting 50 chirps per minute into a cricket formula yielded a temperature of only 52 degrees. Even within crickets, there are different formulas, depending on the species.

Listening to the continuous call of insects can be another way of "counting sheep" to fall asleep, or to determine the temperature. One researcher counted a tree cricket which chirped 2,640 times without stopping.

Nighthawks & Flying Ants

From mid-August to mid-September, common nighthawks, which nest throughout the United States and most of Canada, migrate through the Great Lakes area on their way to South America.

Nighthawks are not actually hawks, as we commonly refer to large birds of prey, but are nighttime insect eaters. As with many birds in the fall, nighthawks tend to flock together. Alice Kelly reports in her book, *Birds of Southeastern Michigan and Southeastern Ontario*, that 5,420 birds were counted on September 7, 1974 from three stations.

Nighthawks are about 10 inches long, gray-brown, with long pointed wings, which have a noticeable white bar not far from the tip.

They have very wide mouths with rictal bristles, or whiskers, protruding from the base of the mouth, which help them detect insects.

Active in evening hours, nighthawks can be seen flying overhead near business districts, feeding on insects attracted to the lights. Business districts also provide nesting sites in the form of flat pea gravel roofs.

Often nighthawks are heard before they are seen. While flying, they emit a nasal *beeeent* sound that is characteristic, and reminiscent, of the *beeeent* of a male woodcock.

In 1986, when returning home from work on a day in mid-August, I noticed a group of about 15 nighthawks feeding by my neighbor's house. It was a rewarding experience, because the birds

A nighthawk chasing insects.

were flying only 10 feet off the ground. They were so busy feeding they allowed my wife, daughter and me to approach within a few feet. We could see the prominent white bar on each wing very clearly and even the barred pattern on the breast.

This group of migrants was attracted to ants emerging from the lawn. Large, winged, fertile female ants were flying into the air, soon to be followed by smaller winged male ants, who will mate with the flying females. Since ants are not aerialists, they were easy prey for the proficient nighthawks. I've often wondered how they actually discovered the ants were there.

During this season, female ants that successfully mate will find a suitable nest site to start a new colony of ants. Mated females will lay eggs, feed the young and care for them until they mature. Then the workers they produce will tend to most of the nest duties.

A few years later I watched 25-30 large dragonflies take advantage of this same phenomenon. Small red colored ants were taking flight and were casually rising from the ground. They reminded me of hot air balloons because they seemed to just float upward. Their lack of controlled flight made them easy targets for the dragonflies.

Concentrated sources of easily obtained food can attract animals of many different kinds. A casual observation of some birds flying and some insects circling resulted in double treats. I probably would not have noticed the mating flights of the ants if it had not been for the predators feeding on them.

Spiders In A Queen Anne's Lace
Looking For Crabs

One of the simple but interesting activities I do with people while walking through fields in late summer is to have them look for crab spiders. They are common, colorful, and fairly easy to find. The first person to find one gets my undying gratitude, or some other nebulous prize.

Searching for crab spiders is best when goldenrod and Queen Anne's lace are blooming. They do not make a web to capture prey; instead they patiently wait for unsuspecting prey on the showy flowerheads of plants.

When an insect searching for nectar or pollen on the flower gets within range for the crab spider, the spider reaches out and grabs it with its very long front legs. Crab spiders are easy to identify because their front two pair of legs are greatly elongated. Most crab spiders have rear pairs of legs which are much shorter. They are used to anchor the spider while it reaches with the longer legs.

Unlike many spiders, the legs of crab spiders extend sideways or perpendicular to the long axis of the body. Because crabs have a similar leg orientation these spiders were similarly named.

As you investigate several flowers along the trail you will notice that the white spiders are on the Queen Anne's lace and the yellow spiders are on the goldenrod. Like a chameleon, some crab spiders can change their body color to match their surroundings.

This ability to change color is advantageous to a spider for a couple of reasons. Camouflage for the crab spider prevents it from being seen by potential prey, and also by predators that would eat the crab spider.

Finding your first crab spider may be the most difficult, but after the first one you will spot them more easily. If you happen to find two crab spiders of very different size on the same flower, you have found a male and a female. Males are much smaller than females.

There are many things that one can watch for and investigate while walking trails. Next time out try looking for crab spiders and note the delicate beauty of the flowers they frequent.

Hawkwatchers of Autumn

Autumn is the time when nature prepares for winter. Many insects lay eggs or develop into larva that will rest all winter long. Frogs will soon bury themselves under a log, or in the soft mud of a pond, to await spring. Monarch butterflies and many species of birds leave the harsh northern climate and migrate south to spend the winter.

Thousands of birds follow the Great Lakes shorelines as they make their way to South America. En route, they pass over Holiday Beach Conservation Area, south of Amherstburg, Ontario, on the Detroit River.

The broad-winged hawk migrates through this area from northern Canada in impressive numbers. Peak numbers are reached in mid-September when thousands congregate overhead. Despite their three-foot wingspans, it is difficult to see them without binoculars.

High in the sky are large, swirling circles of hawks called "kettles." Birds form kettles in order to gain altitude by rising on the upward currents of air formed by changes in the earth's surface. Several hundred birds can be seen in each kettle, and several kettles can be seen in the sky.

They gain altitude at Amherstburg so they can soar across the narrow connection between Canada and the U.S., thus avoiding the long span of Lake Erie which provides little or no rising air currents.

Morning is the best time to see large numbers of birds moving through. I remember one morning several years ago when I saw about 13,000 hawks go by within three hours. The record up to this time is **95,499** broad-winged hawks seen on September 15, 1984.

In addition to the high kettles of broad-winged hawks, there are smaller hawks that migrate closer to the ground. Sharp-shinned hawks and kestrels can be seen regularly.

During fall months, hawk watchers around the U.S. congregate at several places where the birds have been migrating for several thousand years. In 1984, 5,000 people visited Hawk Mountain near Kempton, Penn., on one weekend to watch these magnificent birds pass by.

It's amazing that this phenomenon involving such large numbers of such large birds has been going on for years, yet most people are unaware of this spectacle.

I REMEMBER ONE MORNING SEVERAL YEARS AGO WHEN I SAW ABOUT 13,000 hAWkS GO by WiThiN ThREE hOURS.

Schoolyards & Study Areas
Beyond The Textbooks

In Webster's Third New International Dictionary, natural history was defined as *a former branch of knowledge embracing the study, description and classification of natural objects*. Specialization of many natural history studies probably led Webster and its writers to use the word *former* in their definition. But despite the trend to specialization, which has yielded valuable information, an overall picture of our natural world is also very important.

Specialized sciences, such as botany, ornithology, biochemistry and others, have produced some very detailed results. But getting lost in those details is the danger of specialization. The solution is to integrate details from all the studies into the "big picture."

Natural history is not just facts gleaned from textbooks and journals, but it incorporates personal field experiences that come from contact with the natural world. Field experiences stimulate all the senses and enable the observer to integrate factors that cannot be perceived while reading a textbook.

If we only get our knowledge of the natural world from textbooks, we miss the emotional and aesthetic component of field experiences. Walking under the canopy of century-old beech trees incites a feeling of grandeur that comes only from personal experience. Coming face to face with a white-tailed deer or any wild animal can impregnate in your mind an indelible image.

It is these personal experiences coupled with textbook knowledge that instills a fascination, an appreciation and love for the natural world. Love does not come from textbooks alone. And once you love something, you try and keep it.

The value of this approach to nature study and the development of a "land ethic education" was recognized by the 84th Michigan Legislature. In 1987, it passed Public Act 147 which provides for mechanisms to incorporate nature study into the state's education curriculum. It encourages the use of natural areas with different habitats to teach relationships within the natural community. In a study area, the students would become aware of man's past and present impact on the land. School districts are encouraged to involve students and parents in the use of the site.

A nature study area can be used by students to integrate all the subjects they normally study in the classroom, yet they would be experiencing the natural world first hand. Maintaining natural areas in which students can participate in these studies is the job of progressive communities.

Ageless Recycling

Managing the finances of any business or household comes down to a basic concept - your outgo cannot exceed your income. Many people and governments fail to abide by this maxim and run into trouble.

What is true with man and his attempt to keep his checkbook balanced can also be found in nature. A basic principle of nature is a cycling system. It is one reason why the world has existed for millions of years. Important elements of nature are not consumed and destroyed. They are recycled for use in some other way, thus ensuring that outgo can never exceed income.

Water is a prime example. Dinosaurs may have drunk the same water you are drinking (isn't that a sobering thought?). That is because no new water is being produced; it is only being recycled.

Sunlight causes water to evaporate in an invisible state. Concentrations of water vapor form into clouds, and later it rains back to Earth.

There are many more cycles in nature such as the carbon, oxygen and life cycles. Although business and nature seem like opposite ends of a spectrum, they have many similarities. Just as there is a management hierarchy in business, so is there a hierarchy in social animals. Each individual is well aware of its place in the social structure, though no one wears a sign stating that position. Some of the most stable companies are very diversified, so that if one market should decline, another subsidiary will help to maintain stability. And if one faction should go defunct, its impact on the company would be less than if it were the only faction.

Stable communities in nature are also those that are the most diverse. Forests with different species of trees and levels will support greater varieties of animals because there are more types of food and different kinds of shelter available. If one species of tree should become extinct due to a disease, there will be an impact, but it will be less than if it were a monoculture of corn, for instance.

Man and nature are governed by the same laws of the universe, which accounts for many of the similarities, and since nature has been around much longer than man, important lessons can be learned by examining its methods.

DINOSAURS MAY HAVE DRUNK THE SAME WATER YOU ARE DRINKING... ISN'T THAT A SOBERING THOUGHT?

The Cranes Of Waterloo

As summer's end draws near, the season's crop of young birds begins to flock together. They join with their adults in preparation for flying south before winter.

Migration to southern climes is an annual event that has continued for thousands of years. Most of our summer residents only come north to nest and raise young. Once that is complete, they fly to Florida, Louisiana, or even South or Central America.

Birds from northern Canada will join our Midwest migrants as they start their long southern journey. Many songbirds - warblers, sparrows, thrushes and blackbirds - will follow landmarks such as the Great Lakes, using them like we use a road map.

Several places along the way serve as gathering places where the birds congregate before proceeding. Pt. Pelee in southern Ontario is one of those places.

A variety of birds, as well as monarch butterflies, concentrate at the point, which is the shortest distance from points of land across Lake Erie, and wait for suitable weather before proceeding.

Michigan Audubon Society's Haehnle Sanctuary about 27 miles west of Ann Arbor, Michigan is another great place to watch for migrating birds in fall. The site is on Seymour Road, a mile west of Race Road (exit 147 from I-94). This is where sandhill cranes from the surrounding area and northern Canada congregate before heading south to Florida.

During the day cranes feed in surrounding farm fields but just before sunset hundreds of them fly into the marsh sanctuary near the Waterloo Recreation Area.

Sandhill cranes stand five feet tall and have a wingspan of more than six feet. They fly with their necks extended straight forward, often in long line formations.

The only observation point of the sanctuary is strategically located on a hill, so you can see the birds as they land in the marsh to the east. About 4 p.m. on an average day in October, the birds begin arriving in flocks of five to 150. They approach the marsh from all directions - some will even fly directly overhead.

They approach low enough so you can see the red patch on their foreheads and the gray color of the body feathers. Often times though, even before you see them you can hear the resonant chortle call of the birds as they communicate with each other.

Although the birds are large and you can see them very easily with the naked eye, bring a pair of binoculars so you can see some of the other species of wildlife in the marsh. Several species of ducks and geese can be seen feeding in the open marsh water. White-tailed deer are often seen on the edges of the marsh, too.

Its hard to beat a beautiful fall day in the country at sunset with majestic sandhill cranes saturating your senses.

Nature Through A Raindrop
Take A Closer Look

When deaf people are fitted with a machine that allows them to hear, it is as though a new world has been discovered. When glasses or surgery allow a person with poor eyesight to see clearly, that person has renewed vigor.

Imagine what it was like in 1590 when the Dutch lens maker Zacharias Janssens developed the first microscope. Using this new tool, scientists were able to see a world of micro-organisms that were unknown to them. Since that time, these micro-organisms have become very important in our lives.

Though most people do not have access to a microscope, many often own magnifying lenses. With just an inexpensive hand lens, you too can investigate a whole new world right in your backyard.

In some cases, you may not even need a lens. After the next rain, take some time to examine a drop of water resting on a leaf. A drop of water bends the light and magnifies the image just like a hand lens. Maybe Janssens noticed the same thing and fashioned a piece of glass so it curved like a raindrop and magnified the image. Many things in the natural world have served as inspiration to man's benefit.

While examining the raindrop on a leaf, notice how it enlarges the faint veination seldom seen. These veins carry fluid to each cell just as our veins carry blood. Some decayed leaves show just their skeletal veination, which is the last part to decompose.

With your magnifying glass in hand, look at some soil from your yard. Soil consists of organic material like decayed leaves and inorganic material like pieces of rock. In combination they provide a substratum, which will support life. Dirt, on the other hand, is what you get on the wall, or those little fuzzies you find under your bed.

Small rock particles will show characteristic shapes and forms, depending on their crystalline structure. You may even find a small insect while looking with your hand lens.

Other subjects to explore are small seeds that develop from summer flowers. Many have minute hooks that are designed to attach to fur or to clothing. When you examine them, you will be surprised to see the number of seeds produced and how very small and delicate they are.

IN SOME CASES, YOU MAY NOT EVEN NEED A LENS. AFTER THE NEXT RAIN, TAKE SOME TIME TO EXAMINE A DROP OF WATER RESTING ON A LEAF.

Many subjects can be investigated with a simple hand lense - insects, a feather, or pollen of a flower. Just take the time and you can explore a new world by simply looking closely.

Slowing Down To Observe
Taking Time To Sit

Over the years I have suggested to readers that they take advantage of trails through forest and fields. Hiking is better than biking when it comes to really seeing natural subjects. Slowly traversing the trails allows the observer to travel at his or her own rate, stopping to look and listen whenever at will.

Walking into a forest or natural area is the preferred method, but after arriving, take time to sit and watch. Spending time in the natural world does not mean you have to hike every minute. In fact, sitting is one of the most effective methods of observing.

Although you cover more ground hiking, everything is moving in relation to you. If everything is moving, it is more difficult to detect the movement of other animals. In addition, it is hard not to make noise that can be detected by animals long before you arrive in the area.

Sitting allows you to relax after an invigorating hike and study an area thoroughly. It's surprising how many things can be observed by sitting and watching. Because you are stationary it is easier to detect any movement made by animals. That little moth that flutters by, or the titmouse silently searching rolled leaves for a juicy pupa inside, would likely have gone undetected if you had been moving.

Sounds come alive when you sit and listen. Scolding squirrels, screeching jays and flutters of feathers jump out at you while you

The best birding comes from sitting quietly.

sit. Instead of hearing the warning calls of animals announcing your presence, ordinary sounds of daily activity can be heard.

Sitting allows time to just think about what is around you. Watching for branches and fallen logs while walking can distract your thoughts from more insightful contemplations. There are no signs, lights, people or cars to distract your attention from the beauty of the natural world in front of you.

Fatty Foods For The Feeder
Preparing For Winter

Fall is when living things in the northern temperate regions of the world prepare for the rigors of winter. Man puts antifreeze in the radiator of the car, buys long underwear and puts storm windows on the house.

Wild animals, in their own ways, are also in the process of preparing for winter. Because insects are hard to find in winter, birds that feed on them prepare to migrate south where it is warmer and insects are still available.

But to fly there, birds must store enough energy for the long hard flight. Before birds begin moving to their winter quarters, they may add up to 50 percent more of their body weight in fat. Though many birds feed en route to replenish their energy reserves, many others fly such long distances that even a full stomach could not sustain them very long.

Fat is an excellent source of energy because it provides needed calories over a long period of time. Without it, birds would not be able to fly the long distances required.

Animals that hibernate, such as the meadow jumping mouse and the 13-lined ground squirrel, add as much as 100 percent of their body weight in fat. Even though their body functions are reduced to a bare minimum, they need this fat to keep those functions going during the seven months when they do not eat.

Much of the fat accumulated by hibernating animals is a high energy fat, called brown fat. It provides more energy than the usual saturated fats of animals.

In general, plants have unsaturated fats that remain liquid at lower temperatures than the saturated fats found most often in animals.

Animals that hibernate add as much as 100 percent of their body weight in fat even though body functions are reduced to a minimum.

But animals that live in cold climates have both types in their body. Unsaturated fats are found in the lower portions of the body extremities. Since hooves and paws must remain pliable in cold temperatures, that is where unsaturated fats are found.

Farmers have known for a long time that neatsfoot oil, extracted from the feet of cattle, helps to keep leather boots flexible in cold temperatures.

Though fat is not something man wants too much of in our culture, it serves a necessary function in both man and wild animals. Providing fat-rich foods at a feeder, like suet and sunflower seeds, helps animals maintain their levels of fat, and provide energy for their activities.

Inching Along With Crankerworm Moths

Though I've walked my grandfather's woods near Gaylord, Michigan many times through the years, I never find it boring. Each change in the season alters my perception of the same trees that were there the last time I walked by.

Surprises are one reason I enjoy walking through fields and forests. I never know when I may flush a grouse or spook a deer. One surprise in my grandfather's woods occurred in late November. It had turned cold suddenly, and three inches of snow had fallen. Much of the snow was still plastered to the north side of the trees.

Despite the cold and snow, I found a number of brown, cryptically colored moths clinging to the lee side of the trees.

On practically every tree in the center of the forest, there was at least one moth. Many trees had clusters of 30 or 40 near their bases.

I thought it was unusual to see so many moths at once, and certainly unusual to see insects under such extreme conditions.

As I later discovered, they were all male cankerworm moths, which were ready to mate. Only the male moths have wings which, even when extended, could be covered by a quarter. Females are wingless and very inconspicuous on the bark of a tree. They resemble a dragonfly nymph.

All the males in the woods were waiting for the females to ascend the tree, where they would lay their eggs on the topmost branches.

In spring, the eggs will hatch and the larvae begin feeding on young, emerging leaves.

The cankerworm larvae, or caterpillars, don't have as many legs in the middle of their bodies as most caterpillars. So when they move, their bodies form a loop as their tail ends move forward to meet the front end. Thus their nickname: "loopers" or "inchworm."

When the cankerworm moves, its body forms a loop. Thus their nickname: "loopers" or "inchworm."

After eating their fill of tender leaves, they lower themselves to the ground on gossamer strands. Transformation to an adult moth occurs underground in about four to six weeks.

I recall seeing larvae suspended in space as I walked through the woods during the spring, but I never took the time to follow the life cycle of this creature. This winter experience prompted me to learn more about this hardy moth.

When you find a surprise in the field, take the time to learn about what you saw. It will often teach you more than you ever realized.

HiGh FlyiNG ChipMuNks

Most people maintain their possessions in an orderly manner and behave in a manner consistent with society and their own habits. At breakfast, cereal is in a certain cupboard, fruit is on the counter in a basket, milk is in the refrigerator, and so on. Or we follow a routine upon arriving at work.

As long as everything stays the same, we pay little attention to anything because we have been conditioned to this consistency. However, if something should be out of place, that will make us stand up and notice.

People who watch wildlife come to expect animals to do certain things, too. Chickadees can be expected to be one of the first birds to discover a new feeder. Crab spiders lie in wait for an insect to land close enough for an attack.

And chipmunks are usually seen on the ground - or so I thought. My impression of this striped squirrel of campground fame was a busy, ground-dwelling rodent. It builds tunnels to underground chambers and stores food underground for the winter. So, I thought it should be on the ground.

But during the fall of 1988 I saw chipmunks in tree hollows 15 feet high. Then later in the season I watched one gather acorns from the branches of an oak about 20 feet up.

The branch it was feeding on was over water, and occasionally an acorn would fall. They sounded like little bullets entering the water. I also thought of what might happen if the chipmunk

T. NOWICKI

accidentally slipped.

This chipmunk was carrying at least three medium-sized acorns - one tucked into each cheek pouch and one in front held by its incisors.

After each mouthful it scampered down the tree and bounced across the grass to its burrow. Here it would store the acorns until it awoke for a mid-winter snack.

Its behavior attracted my attention because it seemed so out of place, though it looked as if the chipmunk had done it before. Obviously this kind of behavior is not new to the animal, only to me. Watching wildlife can provide personal discoveries at any time.

The Sense Of Smell
The Scrapes of Autumn

When the Christmas shopping season comes, so come the perfume advertisements. Each company tries to demonstrate, in its own way, that its product is the most alluring.

Although man is predominantly a visual animal, he still relies heavily on hearing and, to a lesser degree, on olfaction to sense the world around him. Over the years, man's sense of smell has been greatly reduced in the tradeoff for a large brain.

In the animal world, smell provides much more knowledge than the approach of danger. Just as significantly, it informs animals about the reproductive status of prospective mates and the territorial boundaries of neighbors.

Moths and butterflies rely on pheromones, a perfume-like chemical, which is emitted to attract the opposite sex. A female moth sits and waits for a male to come to her alluring scent. The male's large, feathery antennae are able to detect minute concentrations of the very specific pheromone, amidst all the other chemicals and pheromones in the air. Some moths can detect their species specific pheromone from as far away as five miles.

Unlike man, other mammals are reproductively receptive only during a short period of time. Chemicals released by the female and smelled by the male inform him of her receptiveness.

White-tailed deer produce a buck rub by scraping the bark off a sapling while removing the velvet from their antlers. Several additional scrapes are made even after the velvet is off. In addition to the physical damage of the tree, the scraping also leaves a scent on the tree from a gland on their foreheads. Though this scent goes unnoticed by man, other bucks passing by recognize that they are entering the territory of another male.

Bucks also move away leaves and debris from an area on the forest floor with their front hooves. This area of exposed dirt is called a *scrape*. It serves both as a visual signal to other deer and an olfactory signal. Chemicals from the urine and scent glands on the back legs are deposited in the scrape to serve as information for other deer.

> Though this scent goes unnoticed by man, other bucks passing by recognize they are entering the territory of another male.

Hikers walking a trail have probably smelled what they thought was a skunk. It was more likely the scent marking left by a fox. Red fox will urinate or defecate in particular places to mark the boundaries of their territories. This scent is discernable by other fox, who know that crossing that invisible boundary line may be dangerous.

Man's sense of smell is not as sensitive as other mammals', but it still functions as an active stimulus to our behavior - as the multi-million dollar perfume industry demonstrates.

Looking For Buried Treasure
Nuts! Where Is It?

Do you know what the most photographed wild animal in America is? According to one federal government survey, it's the squirrel. If you have them in your backyard, you know they are very photogenic and that they can do some pretty amazing things.

Their "tightrope" walking ability along a telephone line, their ability to jump from twig to twig, and their persistence in foiling our anti-squirrel devices are evidence enough that we are dealing with an amazing mammal.

Fall is the time when we often think about these industrious neighbors because they are busy storing nuts for the winter season. Searching a lawn will often reveal several little holes where a squirrel has deposited a nut. Several months later, when fresh food supplies are scarce, they will dig up a nut and eat it.

This is a procedure we are all familiar with, but let's look at this process a little closer. How do they find those nuts that they buried? They don't find all of them, because we have young oak trees sprouting every year, but they do find most.

For many years squirrels were thought to find their food solely by their sense of smell. Mammals have keen senses of smell, and since they buried the nuts, they could leave an odor that would be detectable at a later date. It makes sense, but according a recent study, it's not the only way they find their buried nuts.

They can find their nuts by remembering where they buried

them. It may seem hard for us to believe that such a small animal could remember where its nuts were buried, but that is exactly what the study showed. They memorize the location of the buried nut in relation to local landmarks. If those landmarks are moved, or covered with snow, their retrieval rate is reduced.

Generally, every three years the acorn, or mast crop, is very good. In between years, oaks have moderate to low production of acorns, which means that every nut buried is essential for the animals' survival.

Backyard feeding stations can be very helpful for these furry friends during those lean years. Providing cracked corn, whole corn, or sunflower seeds will help them survive through the cold winter season.

Flocking Around In Fall

Around any town and through the country in late summer and early fall, large flocks of birds are commonly seen. Some flocks consist of only one species, like Canada geese. Other flocks may have two or three species.

Members of the blackbird family are well known for their mixed flocks in fall and winter. Red-winged blackbirds, brown-headed cowbirds, common grackles and starlings can all be seen together in a group at this time of the year.

Large aggregations of birds are very noticeable in fall, not only because of their sizes, but also because they are something different. During spring and summer, most land birds are solitary inhabitants of forest and field. Male birds spend a great deal of time excluding other males from their established territories.

Excluding other birds of the same species from a territory helps ensure adequate food supply for the owner. But in fall, after nesting and raising of young are complete, birds begin to flock together. Decreasing daylight stimulates hormonal changes which allow flocking instead of fighting.

One reason suggested for flocking is to help individuals find food. If one group did not find food after a day of foraging, it may follow a successful flock the next day to find a food supply.

Large groups certainly afford protection from predators. There are more eyes to watch for and detect potential predators for one thing. In addition, individuals in the center of a flock are less likely to be killed by a predator. The larger the flock, the greater chance an individual has of being in the middle.

When a predator does attack a flock of birds flying in loose formation, all the group members close in to form a more compact mass. A falcon or hawk is less able to isolate one bird from the group if they remain close together.

When a hawk does attack a flock in loose formation, the members close in to form a more compact mass, making it hard to isolate one bird.

Not all species of birds flock together. For instance, woodpeckers are very solitary and do not flock. Other species of birds flock at different times of the year, and different age groups of the same species may form flocks at different times.

No matter what the species or time, there are advantages to flocking. Unfortunately at times these aggregations are found too close to man, as some residents can attest to.

Red flashy feathers like those on a red-winged blackbird warns off other birds.

The Reds Of October

Fall is a marvelous time to travel around the Great Lakes to see an overwhelming variety of colors. There are purple asters, white asters, yellow goldenrod, green evergreens and orange maples - as well as many combinations and intensities of each color.

But red objects still attract my attention first. I recall the staghorn sumac leaves in open fields, red maples flashing in the forest and a male cardinal sitting in our magnolia tree.

In nature, red colored structures are usually reserved for warning signals. Scarlet red epaulets (shoulder patches) of red-winged blackbirds are prominently displayed when a male bird encounters another male, but remain covered when they are not needed. Exposing these flashy feathers warns an approaching bird not to come any closer.

Other species of birds have red feathers hidden on top of their heads. Male Nashville warblers, eastern kingbirds, ruby and golden-crowned kinglets all have these red patches that are exposed only when signaling a warning. Constant exposure of these red patches would reduce their impact when it was really needed.

Sticklebacks, small fish with sharp spines on their backs, use red to attract attention and serve as a warning. During the breeding season, a male's belly turns red. If a male defending a territory sees another red-bellied male, he will challenge the intruder.

Experiments have been conducted to demonstrate that it is the color red which actually stimulates the stickleback's aggressive behavior. Models with painted red bellies caused the same response in a male defending his territory. In one instance, a stickleback in an aquarium became aggressive when a red mail truck drove by.

Red structures aren't always warning signals. A red spot on the bill of herring gulls serves as a stimulus and a target which young birds peck at in order to get food from their parents.

Red is the color that initiates this kind of behavior, but only during certain times of the year when it is beneficial for the animal. Warning signals are very effective in reducing the number of actual physical battles between animals; forewarning an approaching animal of possible consequences before it is injured in battle.

Man uses red in similar ways. We have red stop signs, red traffic lights, red fire engines and reddish hunting jackets - all to attract our attention so that we behave appropriately.

Personal Space In A Flock
Birds On A Wire

Fall is the season when the behavior of birds changes from defending territories to gregariousness. Juveniles and adults form large flocks seen frequently around metropolitan areas.

Blackbirds, of three to five different species, constitute most of the conspicuous flocks seen at this time of year.

One day, while driving past a major expressway intersection, I noticed a large flock of birds. They were feeding in the fields and marshes of the cloverleaf, putting on a layer of fat to sustain them on their migration south.

When the birds stopped feeding, they flew to the towers and cables that dissected the intersection. As I passed by I noticed that all the birds on the wires were evenly spaced from their neighbors. From a distance, they looked like inch marks on a ruler.

A few days later at work, I watched a starling land on a telephone wire among a group of neatly spaced birds. When it landed, birds on either side of it moved away to establish the same distance they had between neighbors before it arrived.

Birds next to the two that moved adjusted their spacing, and so it went on down the line, reminding me of a game of dominoes. One reason for individuals to maintain a distance is to ensure adequate room to take flight when necessary.

Individual spacing is readily observed in birds, but not restricted to them. Man too has a "personal space" that he maintains when conditions allow it.

People standing in line adjust the distance between themselves and the people in front of them, particularly strangers, when room permits.

Under crowded conditions, this invisible "bubble" disintegrates, but man then institutes other behavioral actions to compensate for his loss of personal space, like crossing our arms against our chest or saying "excuse me."

Though each person has his own individual distance, take note of the spacing of people in line at the bank next time.

Individual spacing is readily observed in birds, but not restricted to them. Man also needs personal space.

The Traveling Naturalist

Watching wildlife has become a very popular form of recreation. Many travel agencies and conservation groups offer trips to exotic areas where people can see everything from butterflies to belugas.

Expanding your realm of exploration to beyond your backyard is a wonderful way to enhance your appreciation for the diversity of life. Not only will you see the animals most nature photographers concentrate on, you will experience the lesser known creatures that are even more common. Using skills honed from observing in your backyard, you will see both the differences and similarities when viewing life in a new area.

By traveling to new areas you will meet local experts that are often more than willing to share their knowledge of the flora and fauna. Some programs or trips offer formal classes. This is an excellent way to learn about and enjoy the natural world.

One day a friend and I were talking and she reminded me of one of the more special moments I have had birding. It occurred while I was attending a workshop on shorebirds at the University of Maine-Machias. There were several people whose company I enjoyed, but it was definitely the birds that produced an indelible image in my memory.

Time was spend in the classroom reviewing migration routes and shorebird identification, but the time we all waited for was the time in the field. When the tide was out, birds scattered to many exposed shores, which made it difficult to find sufficient numbers of them. So we spent much of our time exploring the high tide roosting areas of migrating shorebirds. When they cannot find food, they gather in groups for safety.

One group we came upon numbered at least 100,000 birds. Most of them were semi-palmated sandpipers, with a few least sandpipers, white-rumped sandpipers and semi-palmated plovers mixed in. Though I had seen all these species before, never had I seen them in such numbers. As we approached, it was hard to actually identify individual birds. Their bodies were shoulder to shoulder with heads tucked down forming a carpet on the beach.

When we approached too closely, the birds nearest our group took flight. Their flying caused the birds next to them to fly, and so it went down the line. It looked like someone lifting a carpet to shake it out.

Watching 100,000 birds take flight and listening to the beating of their wings was an experience in itself to remember. But watching them fly in undulating waves out over the ocean was even more spectacular. As the mass of birds formed a rippling ribbon, wing tip to wing tip, not a single bird fell out of step.

While traveling take advantage of any classes or programs to expand your knowledge of the natural world.

Their illumination by the warm rays of the setting sun added the final sparkle to this experience. As each bird flapped in flight, their wings would interrupt the gleaming white of the setting sun reflected off their bellies. Contrasted against the black ocean water, they looked like twinkling stars moving through space.

The more time you spend in the field, the more chances you will have of encountering memorable experiences. Expanding your realm of interest in natural history to new subjects and areas beyond your backyard will increase your chances even greater.

Bird Feeder Hawks

Those who have been feeding birds for several years have probably had a bird feeder at their bird feeder. If you have not had a bird feeder at your bird feeder, you probably will.

What are bird feeders at your bird feeder? In our area they are typically the sharp-shinned hawk and the Cooper's hawk. They are kissing cousins and can be difficult to separate in the field.

Both species are in the subcategory of hawks known as Accipiters. Accipiters have a long tail and rounded wings used for flying between and around trees in a forest. They use these features to overcome woodland birds which they feed upon.

Sharp-shinned hawks measure 10 to 14 inches from tip of the bill to tip of the tail, Cooper's measure 14 to 20 inches. Females are larger; that is why there is such a range in size. As you can see too, a large sharp-shinned is as long as a small Cooper's.

Coloration in the two species is similar. Adults have a blue-gray back with underparts of red bars on a white background. Juveniles are brown on the back with loose brown stripes running down the front from head to tail. Their body form is narrow compared to the large hawks seen on the side of the highway.

Separating the two species takes practice. In the short time people see a hawk dash in and take a bird from their feeder, they will not be able to identify its species in most cases. If it looks very big it's likely a Cooper's; if it looks very small it's likely a sharp-shinned.

If one of these species does frequent your feeder do not be alarmed. They will probably take a couple birds and then leave to new feeding areas where the birds are not as wary. Its possible they will return in a few weeks or days, but consider it an opportunity to observe a phenomenon that few people get a chance to see, even though we know it happens all the time.

As a consequence of people enjoying birds at feeders, we are also concentrating birds for the bird feeders and providing little buffets for them. According to Detroit Audubon Society Christmas Bird Count data, from 1945-1974 only three sharp-shinned hawks were identified; from 1975-1990 there were 19 sharp-shinned hawks identified. Feeding stations may alter the need to migrate for many individuals because of these numerous buffets. This idea also illustrates why a bird feeding station needs to include adequate cover so birds can escape danger.

Body Burying Beetles
Death And Decomposers

A student recently asked me the life span of some species of birds. She was surprised, as most people are, that small birds like chickadees average only one to two years. Banded birds have been recorded as old as 10 years, but that is not the norm. Slightly larger birds like robins live a couple years longer.

The next question was, if wild animals have such a short life span, why don't we find more dead animals around? This is a very good question and allows us to think about the small, forgotten animals that answer it.

If the natural world did not have the decomposers, as they are called, we would be up to our armpits in waste and dead bodies. Several different kinds of animals help to prevent this.

First, most wild animals are eaten by other animals as food. The atoms and elements from one body are recycled into the predator. What little may be left of the prey animal will be decomposed by bacteria or consumed by insects or other scavengers.

Waste material from a multitude of animals is either a source of nutrients for fungus, bacteria or green plants, or it is buried by dung beetles. Dung beetles use it as a place in which to lay their eggs. Larva feed on the remaining foodstuffs while protected underground from many predators.

Bodies of animals that die of old age may be buried by carrion beetles. They undermine the carcass and bury the body so it is protected from other scavengers. I happened to see a common carrion beetle while walking on the trail one day. It reminded me of their important role in the cycles of nature.

Ants, beetles, flies, bacteria, fungi and scavengers such as shrews, crows, skunk, opossum and raccoon are all part of nature's clean-up crew. If they were not around, I suspect that there would be many more diseases. Their impact can be seen in winter when an animal killed by a vehicle on the road is observed over time. When insects and bacteria are not around, a carcass may persist until warm weather returns.

A corollary of this subject is why are deer antlers rarely found? Deer shed their antlers in mid-winter, but small rodents active all year eat the antlers for their minerals and calcium.

CARRION BEETLES UNDERMINE THE CARCASS AND BURY THE body so it is PROTECTED FROM OTHER SCAVENGERS.

Because they are small, though actually quite numerous, many decomposers go unnoticed, except for their noticeable effects.

That Amazing Squirrel Tail

Body language is a silent form of communication people use every day without even thinking. When we unexpectedly meet an old friend, our eyebrows quickly flick up and then down unconsciously. This movement relays a message of pleasure that is perceived by the friend who does the same to you.

Crossed arms, lowered eyebrows, or a wrinkled nose are just some of the other ways people use body language to communicate with one another.

Animals also use a great deal of body language to communicate. They have vocalizations which are interpreted by others of their species and sometimes by other species. But postures and behaviors communicate more than most realize.

Fox squirrels in our yards communicate frequently with their tails. When their tails are waving in gently arches back and forth, they are usually involved with a member of the opposite sex. It serves to communicate appeasement and intent.

A tail that is being flicked or jerked back and forth abruptly is a sign of alarm. Other squirrels in the area, which are frequently relatives, will see this movement and seek shelter or investigate the situation.

Tail fluffing is a sign of disturbance, or possibly frustration. Subtle changes in the movement of the tail can communicate something very different.

In addition to being a signaling device, a squirrel's tail has several other functions. On sunny days it may serve as a shield to shade the

body from overheating. If it should rain, it can serve to protect the body for a period of time. Protecting the body with its internal organs is very important.

When cold winter weather arrives, squirrels curl up in their leafy nests or tree cavities with their tails wrapped around their head. In this case it serves as a blanket or scarf. Jumping from tree to tree requires precise balance in order to avoid injury. Moving the tail can adjust for balance and direction when needed, like the pole used by tightrope walkers. Similarly, when a squirrel is swimming it can use it's tail as a rudder to adjust for direction, or to capture air and serve as a floatation device.

The most useful kinds of devices are those which serve more than one purpose. Next time you watch a squirrel in your yard, see if you can determine any other uses for their tails.

Whose Nest Is It?
Cowbirds And Warblers

Changes in the natural world are like a baseball pitcher and a batter. A pitcher develops a new pitch that is very effective in striking out batters. So the batter begins to experiment with different ways of counteracting the pitch that will result in a hit. After a period of time, the pitch has lost its effectiveness, and the pitcher must develop another one.

This constant point/counterpoint can also be seen in the natural world. A hawk is trying to capture mice more efficiently, while the mouse is trying to evade hawks more effectively.

In the case of Kirtland's warblers, which nest in only three or four counties in northern Michigan, they have not had time to counteract the parasitism of the brown-headed cowbird. Cowbirds lay their eggs in the nests of other birds and let the host incubate and care for the young.

Historically, cowbirds were found in the plains of North America. It is believed cowbirds followed the buffalo herds and developed their parasitic behavior in response to their nomadic wanderings. Though Michigan did have some native prairies, they did not extend into the northern part of the state where the Kirtland's warbler nests. Then the lumbering era created large open areas.

Cowbirds followed the extension of the plains into Michigan and found the Kirtland's warbler an easy host. Many other birds, approximately 220, are host to the cowbird and raise their young too, but one species is changing.

Yellow warblers have been host to cowbirds for many years. The warblers nest in open shrubby fields where cowbirds can easily see where they are building their nest.

When the nest is complete, a female cowbird will lay an egg in the nest and let the warbler incubate and raise its young. Yellow warblers, though, have begun to recognize when cowbird eggs are in their nest. Unable to remove the egg, the warbler will build another nest on top of the original nest. If a cowbird egg is laid in the second layer, it may build a third layer on top of the second. One nest was discovered with six layers and a cowbird egg in each layer.

When I investigated, there were two layers to the yellow warbler nest. A cowbird egg was still in the lower level.

As I was walking near a marsh one day, I noticed a yellow warbler nest that looked deeper than usual. When I investigated, there were two layers to the nest. A cowbird egg was still in the lower level.

Yellow warblers have now begun to counteract the parasitism of the cowbird. The next move is up to the cowbird.

A red-phase ruffed grouse.

Winter

FACE TO FACE WITH WILDLIFE
PERSONAL ENCOUNTERS

Las Vegas, Atlantic City, lotteries and football pools all thrive on the attraction of gambling. Once a person has won more than he has invested, he's hooked. Sometimes he's hooked before they win more than they have invested! The chance of winning lures people back to try again.

Though winning happens far less often than losing, this does not deter the average person. As I think back on the number of times I have walked through fields and forests, the truly memorable experiences have been few.

But those experiences produced truly indelible memories. One I can recall quite clearly involved an owl. I remember bending forward at the waist to walk through some dense brush, and when I came to an opening and stood up, I was face to feathers with a screech owl. We both looked at each other for an instant and then it decided to find a new place to rest. I have no idea why it did not fly away earlier.

People who enjoy fishing do not always catch a trophy fish, but they catch enough to make the day enjoyable, hoping that the next nibble will be a winner.

Walking through meadows and canoeing down streams are enjoyable pursuits that always serve to brighten the spirits. But the uncertainty of what lies beyond each bend in the trail, or curve in

the river, is like the lure of gambling.

A white-tailed deer may be drinking at the waters edge around that next bend, an otter may be swimming across the river, or a weasel may be searching for a mouse. There may be a cluster of scarlet cardinal flowers blooming by the trail that may distract your eyes from the stump in your path.

Any number of things can cause one hike to be more memorable than another, but like any gambler knows, the more you play the more you win. Actually, hiking is always a winning activity and it does not cost anything to play.

Coats Of Many Colors

Some animals, like gray squirrels and great blue herons, come in two different colors. Gray squirrels may be either gray or black. Great blue herons in the Great Lakes area are typically blue-gray in coloration, but in Florida there are great blue herons that are pure white.

Two common birds in the Great Lakes area that exhibit color phases are the screech owl and the ruffed grouse. Red-phased screech owls are not as common in Michigan as the gray-phase birds. With the ruffed grouse, however, red-phase birds are much more common.

Color phases of these two birds are not seasonal changes which occur in snowshoe hares and ermines. An individual is born either red or gray and stays that color during its entire life. Both colors may be found in the same brood.

Seasonal color changes represent an adaptation to changes in climate in the temperate regions of the world. A white coat grown by ermines and hares in winter is excellent camouflage against snow. Ptarmigan, the Alaska state bird that is also found in northern Canada, changes from a summer brown to a winter white too.

Most animals, however, do not change color from season to season, or even exhibit color phases. Animals typically have the same basic coloration and pattern to their feathers, fur or scales.

Screech owls, on the other hand, are born either red, gray, or a medium brown color. Studies have shown that in the northern part of their range, the gray color predominates. In the southern part of their range, the red phase predominates. Medium brown birds make up a very small portion of the population.

Red-phase birds are unable to assimilate energy as well as gray birds do when weather conditions in northern regions are harsh for several days.

Ruffed grouse, sometimes known as a partridge, also have red, gray and mixed color phases. Like the screech owl, gray-phase grouse are better able to survive the colder temperatures and are more common farther to the north in Canada.

Most animals, however, do not change color from season to season, or even exhibit color phases.

Variations such as these, and many others in the natural world, help to ensure that some individuals will survive when conditions change. A classic example of this occurred during the 1950s in England. Peppered moths occured in a white and gray phase and rested on tree trunks during the day. In the industrial period of the 1950s, white-phase moths that were once the most common began to decline, while the dark-phase moths increased.

As the trees in the country became darkened with soot, white-phase moths resting on soot covered trees were eaten by predators more often than the camouflaged dark-phase moths.

Variation in a population is very important for survival over a long period of time. Differences in individuals may be evident from the outside, or there may be something internally that would allow one individual to survive and not another.

THE WINTER WOODPILE

Cold temperatures do not recognize the official beginning of winter. The season seems to slowly shift, and as early as October we experience winter conditions. Man's time table is artificial.

Regardless of the official season, when the temperature drops it is time to stoke up the wood-burning stove. Splitting logs that were cut a couple years ago is always easier in cold weather. What water is left in the dried log freezes and, when hit with an axe splits, like ice cubes shatter when they fall.

Splitting wood has many advantages and reminds me of Thoreau's statement that went something like ... chopping wood warms the body twice. Even on cold days wielding an axe can work up a sweat, while burning the wood also keeps the body warm.

But I found that my wood pile warms me in other ways. One summer while replacing a fence near my stacked wood, I noticed the transparent capsule of an empty butterfly chrysalis. It could have been from a painted lady, a mourning cloak or maybe even a fritillary. All these species of butterfly have a chrysalis with a saw-tooth edge.

I would like to have seen both the caterpillar and the adult, but I was satisfied that my wood pile provided a safe retreat.

As I shift and sift through the logs at different seasons, evidence of other inhabitants unfolds. Not far from the butterfly chrysalis was a paper wasp nest that had been abandoned the previous year. It too was attached by a single pedicel, which supported an open

The winter wood pile.

umbrella of neatly arranged hexagonal columnar cells.

Attaching their nest in the wood pile was like building a log house in the middle of a forest. Dried wood is the source of the cellulose which when mixed with their saliva, makes paper for the nest. I've often thought that the Chinese were inspired by wasps when they "discovered" paper. These wasps did not have to expend much energy traveling from the source to their nest.

Providing or maintaining habitats for animals is necessary for their survival. Habitats do not always have to be large, but the fact that they allow creatures to exist warms me in addition to the wood.

OBSERVATIONS IN WRITING
THE FIELD JOUNRAL

When an animal finds an abundant source of food it develops a "search image." A search image enables an animal to find a source of food quickly and efficiently. Sometimes the animal may bypass edible food while it is searching for the more abundant food.

One thing is certain: The animals know how to find food because they are observant. Hikers and naturalists can enhance their powers of observation by writing and drawing in a notebook.

Walking trails is enjoyable and fun, but knowing what is along the trail makes it even more enjoyable. Carrying a library of field guides for any possible encounter with wildlife could be a bit too much in the daypack. A lighter alternative is to carry a sketch pad and a notebook to record pertinent information.

If you take the time to stop and sit and sense the surroundings, it is remarkable what you will observe. Writing down what you are viewing, or hearing, or smelling, or feeling, will help to codify the experience. Writing forces one to describe what is there and to put observations into perspective. It also stimulates deeper thoughts.

A written description can be long and flowery, or short and simple. No matter how it is written, be sure to put a date and place notation along with a comment about the weather. This will be helpful to know if comparisons are to be made in the future.

Complementing written descriptions with some drawings or illustrations will enhance a journal remarkably. Drawings do not

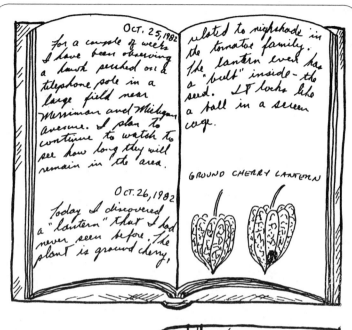

OCT. 25, 1982

For a couple of weeks I have been observing a hawk perched on a telephone pole in a large field near Merriman and Michigan Avenue. I plan to continue to watch to see how long they will remain in the area.

OCT. 26, 1982

Today I discovered a "lantern" that I had never seen before. The plant is ground cherry,

related to nightshade in the tomatoe family. The lantern even has a "bulb" inside - the seed. It looks like a ball in a screen cage.

GROUND CHERRY LANTERN

A journal is the best way to keep observations and thoughts gathered while outdoors.

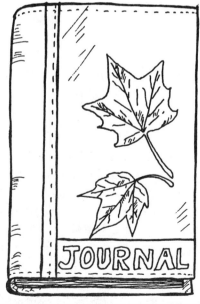

JOURNAL

have to be superior; they are just a means to help learn about a particular subject. Many people feel they cannot draw, but a rough sketch, with descriptions in the margins to supplement your drawing, will provide enough information for future use. Examining a subject closely enough to draw it will only enhance your appreciation and knowledge of the subject. A cursory examination does not define the detail that a more extended observation would.

Doing some sketching will also provide one with a greater appreciation for those professionals who create some marvelous paintings and sculptures of wildlife they have experienced.

Your journal will improve your observations, furnish descriptions for identification later, and provide nostalgic reading in the future.

TRACKS OF A FOX ON THE RUN
A WINTER STORY

Forests and meadows, after a new snowfall, can be like a fairyland. As it was in "The Nutcracker" prince's kingdom, rolling hills look like mounds of sugar, and snow resting on delicate branches creates a lacy network rivaling a single snowflake.

Sunlight glittering on the surface can remind one of a diamond's shimmering facets. And like a diamond, winter is a hard season for wild animals. Yet it allows man to clearly see what animals are doing.

New snow is like the pages of a blank book. Animal tracks add words to those pages, and following those tracks tells a story.

Those animals that do not migrate, hibernate or sleep must continue to find food during the winter. Deep snow may make it hard for animals like squirrels to find nuts on the ground. But deep snow can enable a rabbit to reach twigs and branches that previously were out of reach.

Predators, like the fox, must hunt for the few animals that do remain active all winter. A fox trail is easy to recognize. Its tracks are in a straight line, one in front of the other. Following the necklace trail of a fox can tell the observer how difficult it is to survive in winter.

I followed a fox trail one day, and as the fox casually walked through the snow and jumped onto a fallen log, one could imagine its nose testing the air for the scent of an animal.

Or as the track paralleled another fallen log, how the fox searched for an unsuspecting mouse. Its tracks may be in a single file, but its trail scattered to every potential source of food.

New snow is like pages of a good book and following animal tracks tells the story.

Then, along the trail the tracks became clustered together. All four feet were poised next to each other. Just ahead there must have been a mouse scurrying under the snow. After a moment of orientation, the fox leaped two feet through the air and landed with all four feet and its face in the snow.

It looked as though the mouse escaped, because there were more tracks in the snow and more holes where the fox had pushed its nose in to find the mouse.

Though not a fairy tale, the activities of wild animals are vividly exposed in the winter snow - if you take the time to read.

A Sudden Taste For Sunflower
Bird Feeder Behavior

Throughout time animals have adapted to particular places or habitats. Their physical features and behavior have been modified so they can sustain life within the limitations of climate and the habitat. Song frequency and bill length of birds, for example, are best suited for where they live and what food is available to eat.

Animals that have the best methods of getting food or avoiding predators are going to survive. Over time, each individual of a species will be seen using the same efficient methods of survival. But in order for a species to survive over time, it must also have some flexibility in its behavior, and some variation in its physical features, to accommodate to unexpected changes.

At this time no major changes in wildlife have occurred as a result of the extensive network of feeding stations throughout the United States. But I think some changes are occurring gradually.

Tree sparrows that come south in winter from their northern Canada nesting grounds are one of the most predictable ground feeders I know. If they are not feeding on the ground, they are only a few feet above the ground on a platform feeder, or so I thought.

One day while watching birds at a feeder, to my surprise, I saw a tree sparrow perched on a tube feeder pecking at sunflower seeds. Not only was it unusual to see it perched on such a feeder, but a sparrow does not typically eat sunflower seeds.

Mourning doves, which I associate as a ground feeder can now be seen investigating hanging tube feeders and other feeders off the ground.

Both these birds are exhibiting behavior that I consider atypical, and it makes me wonder. Maybe my conception of their behavior is incomplete, or maybe their behavior is changing.

Birds are very visual animals and watch other birds feeding at bird feeders. It seems very plausible to me that tree sparrows and mourning doves would investigate to see what other birds are eating. They would even try to eat what other birds find acceptable.

Sunflower seeds are a good source of energy in winter and are commonly used at many feeding stations. Because they are eaten by so many different birds, any bird at a feeding station could not help but be attracted to them.

As bird feeders continue to be a source of food, it will be interesting to note if these behaviors become more ingrained and if new behaviors develop.

> The bird behavior was atypical and made me wonder; were my conceptions incomplete or was their behavior changing.

Polevaulting Chickadees

Often times common things become trite. House sparrows are very common, and in combination with their less than-striking plumage, are not one of the most beloved birds in the area. Even desirable birds like the chickadee lose their newness as they frequent feeders day after day.

One way to keep the freshness in watching wildlife is to watch for new and unseen behaviors. Behavior watching adds new dimensions to common species. Watching house sparrows can become interesting if you learn to watch for courtship, aggressive postures, or territorial disputes.

One winter I got to watch some interesting feeding behavior of the black-capped chickadee. I was with a class near Houghton Lake, Michigan, walking along a seldom used country road. While scanning the trees I spotted a red squirrel nest and I saw where a porcupine had been eating the bark off a red pine. When my eyes focused back down the road I saw some bird activity ahead.

As we approached them I realized they were chickadees, but they were oblivious to our presence. They were more concerned with feeding on the winter flowerheads of bergamot. Bergamot has an upside down bowl shaped flowerhead on top of a long thin square stem. Even the light weight of a chickadee could not be supported by the thin stem.

So the chickadees flew to the flowerhead and grabbed hold of the stem with their feet. Their weight bent the stem in an arch to

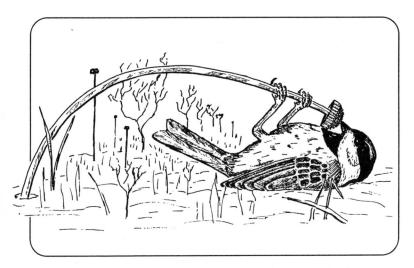

the ground, with the chickadee holding on. Now on its back, resting on the snow and holding on to the stem, the chickadee probed the many tubes that held seeds in the flowerhead. It reminded me of a pole vaulter whose pole had been planted and was about to be propelled up over the bar.

When they had finished probing and feeding they would let go of the stem, which sprang back to an upward position, and then fly to another flowerhead. Impressed in the snow were the marks of the bird's back and wing feathers from when they took flight. This common bird feeding in this manner was new and exciting to me.

NUTHATCH INVASION

The winter of 1989-90 was the season of the red-breasted nuthatch. Many people who feed birds told me they had a new nuthatch at their feeder. Most observers were quite familiar with the white-breasted nuthatch, so they knew when a new species appeared.

Both the white and red-breasted nuthatches forage by going down a tree trunk head first. Unlike woodpeckers and creepers who orient themselves with their heads up and spend most of their time going up a tree, nuthatches view from a different perspective and find food other birds missed.

They are similar in their coloration too. A blue-gray back with black to dark gray on the top of their head is a common coloration to both. But the red-breasted nuthatch is slightly smaller, has a black line through the eye separating white above and below, and has reddish underparts.

Red-breasted nuthatches typically nest in the northern part of Michigan in coniferous forests of spruce, pine and fir. Occasionally nests have been found in the southern tier of counties. They excavate a cavity in a dead tree and smear pine resin around the opening. It is believed that it keeps some predators from entering the nest. Some experiments have shown that snakes are deterred by pine resin.

When a red-breasted nuthatch is seen around the Detroit area it is considered a good sighting because they do not stay around this part of the state. But there are years when the cone production in the coniferous forests is low, which causes irruptions of this species in new areas as they search for food.

Most years reveal a few birds in southeastern Michigan, but some years, like 1957, 1969, 1975 and 1989 indicated a greater number than usual. The 1989 Detroit Audubon Society's Christmas Bird Count recorded the greatest number of red-breasted nuthatches in its 45-year history.

Regular counts like this and those sponsored by the federal government help us monitor trends in bird populations on a broad scale. In some cases, these same trends can be seen at your feeders.

Owls At The Airport

Snowy owls fly south periodically in winter from their tundra nesting grounds in Canada when their food supply is low. This periodic movement allows people in the upper Midwest to see a species of bird they would normally have to travel hundreds of miles to see.

Even when miles from their normal habitat, visiting snowy owls choose places to hunt which are similar to their nesting grounds. Short grass fields and beaches are two common areas to look for them.

Airports are also great places to watch for snowy owls. The short grass of the runways and surrounding areas is reminiscent of their tundra hunting grounds.

While driving by Metropolitan Airport outside Detroit on my

way to work one day, I saw a snowy owl fly across the expressway toward the terminal buildings. I made a quick loop around the airport, but failed to spot it again.

At lunch I drove around the airport, looking at light poles and fence posts for a large, white protrusion. Then I circled the terminal buildings.

It may seem incongruous to look for a northern nomad of the barren tundra around a busy airport, but as I was about to head back to work, I looked up at an antenna protruding from the roof of the U.S. Postal Service building - and there it was. Perched on the top of this long, thin pole was a very streaked snowy owl.

THE SHORT GRASS OF THE AIRPORT RUN-WAYS IS REMI-NISCENT OF THE TUNDRA HUNTING GROUNDS OF SNOWY OWLS.

Birds with heavy streaking of their plumage are believed to be juveniles. Young birds are inexperienced and cannot defend or maintain a territory against older birds when food supplies are low.

Another oddity was the high promontory on which the bird was perched. Tundra habitat in northern Canada lacks vegetation more than a few feet above ground.

Yet this bird, and others that are seen outside their typical tundra habitat, quickly learn to take advantage of high hunting perches. From a high vantage point, it could not only see mice and voles in the field, but wink at passengers of incoming flights.

All animals and plants are adapted for certain habitats and remain in those areas whenever possible. Some animals are able to adapt to similar habitats if they are displaced. Others, with more rigid requirements, will die if displaced. Even during temporary displacements - such as migration - animals seek familiar habitats.

When Field Indentification Fails
What Species Is It?

A common statement made by people new to birding and bird identification is that the bird in the field doesn't look like the picture in the book. Well, there can be a lot of truth to that statement.

First of all, artists that paint the portraits of birds in field guides must select a representative bird from a vast collection. If one could see a large collection of museum specimens, the variation in coloration and patterns would be very noticeable - but within a tolerable range.

Just as no two people are exactly alike, so it is with birds. And the bird you see in the field, or at your feeder, may not look just like the one the artist chose to paint.

Identifying basic patterns, shapes, and physical structures will allow one to correctly identify a bird, but try not to be discouraged because it does not look exactly like the book.

There are times when one has to go by experience to identify some really unusual birds. A woman once wrote me that she had a white bird with black in its wings at her feeder. She said it was the size of a sparrow and had been feeding at her feeders for days.

If one looked in the field guide and tried to identify a bird with those features, the most likely bird would be a snow bunting. Buntings at feeders are very unlikely, though.

Since it was not far from home I decided to take a look at the

bird myself. After comparing its size, bill shape, behavior and general profile with the house sparrows it was associating with, I felt certain it was an almost completely white house sparrow. It was not a true albino because it did have some brown spots and a wash of brown under its bill. A true albino would not have any traces of brown or color, and it would have a red eye.

Positive identification of a rare coloration like this is based on the shape of the bird, its behavior and its associates. Albinos, or nearly white birds, are easy to spot but can be confusing to identify.

One day I saw a mourning dove that had several white feathers on its back. If one were unfamiliar with the general appearance of a normal dove, one may think it was a new species. Damage to the skin where the feathers emerge can cause white feathers in patches rather than all over like the house sparrow.

A good example of that occurred when a bird rehabilitator could not identify the adult bird she had rescued. It looked like a sparrow but it had a tail that was completely white. Field guides show no such bird. When I looked at the bird, all the features indicated a song sparrow, except for the tail. During its development it must have injured the base of the tail causing the feathers to emerge white instead of brown.

White spotting occurs more commonly than true albinism and can cause confusion, but it forces birders to check several other features in order to identify it properly.

Winter Clicker

Few insects bother us in winter because after the first frost of fall, insects are seldom seen.

Their small sizes and body chemistry do not allow them to maintain a warm body in cold air temperatures. In preparation for winter, adult insects may lay eggs that overwinter. Then the adults die.

Praying mantis egg cases are common on winter weeds in the meadows across the Midwest. They look like a piece of hardened spray foam that has wrinkles like an accordion.

Some insects overwinter in an immature stage of their life cycle. Dragonfly eggs develop into nymphs that will feed on small aquatic life under water. Depending on the availability of food, they may be under water for more than one winter. When the nymph is ready, it will crawl up a reed stem above the water and transform into an adult dragonfly.

Some insects can overwinter as adults - such as the mourning cloak and tortoise shell butterflies. Even though these insects may remain as adults, they are seldom seen, except when a warm spell arrives in mid-winter.

That was when we found a click beetle walking across the kitchen floor. My 2-year-old son found it interesting while it moved along lethargically.

After examining the dark brown, three-quarter-inch long insect with rounded ends, I decided to show my son and daughter why they call it a "click beetle." I gently picked the insect up and placed it on its back on the floor. When the click beetle finds itself in this position, it will arch upward, then push down forcibly which produces a click sound. Pushing down propels the insect about six inches into the air. While in the air the insect rights itself so its feet are pointing down. Most of the time the click beetle lands on its feet. Each time it flipped, my son and daughter laughed at the performance.

This little interlude of natural history on the kitchen floor taught my children more than just how a click beetle jumps. It showed them that insects can be interesting. They do not have to be stepped on whenever they are discovered inside a house. Most insects would rather be outside where they belong. A preservation approach to something like an insect in the house can help instill the proper attitude toward living things in their natural environment.

The Commuter Naturalist

As I travel to work each day I enjoy searching for wildlife at several different locations. Traveling the same route everyday allows me the opportunity to note changes and to search likely areas for wildlife.

When I pass Heritage Park, I always search the pond for geese, herons, ducks and other animals. One summer, I frequently saw a belted kingfisher on the windmill frame. The framework provided a clear view to the pond below where it searched for fish.

Unfortunately, I also saw a dead red fox near the entrance once. This happened during the summer when females were feeding young. It would have been unfortunate if that animal was the female who had to feed young at a den I discovered in the park. Those young surely would have died.

Farther north along my route I keep my eyes open for birds at a new storm water retention facility. In spring, when birds are migrating through the area, the saturated mud and shallow water should provide good habitat for shorebirds. I'd need to scan the area with a spotting scope to really see what is there, but when I pass by I can at least identify any activity.

One of my best places to see wildlife is an open field with adjacent woodlots and a wetland. This place often provided my first red-winged blackbird of the year. They were attracted to the willows and cattails associated with the wetland.

LEARNING TO SCAN LIKELY PLACES FOR WILDLIFE WHILE DRIVING CAN HAVE ITS REWARDS.

In the forest, after the leaves had dropped, I could see abandoned hawk nests along the edge. One spring day I watched a red-tailed hawk carrying a stick in its talon for repair of an old nest. Those abandoned nests should be good for great horned owls to nest in, though I had not seen any.

I enjoy watching for adult red-tailed hawks perched on the branches of a dead tree along the edge of the forest. Several mornings when I drive by they are in the same place facing in the same direction. They seem to have an agenda just as I do on my way to work.

This same area provided two very good observations just a few weeks apart. My first observation was of a red fox sitting next to a pile of dirt watching traffic pass by. Then a couple weeks later I saw what I thought was a mink dash into the grass. Wetlands are perfect places for mink to hunt.

Learning to scan likely places for wildlife, while driving - and in between keeping an eye out for wild cars and even wilder drivers - can have its rewards.

Caddisfly Cover-up

During warm days of March when the ice melts on fast-flowing streams, take a look into the water. Looking into the clean, clear water one day, I could see the bottom. Though the stream was not deep, the water was exceptionally clear.

Cold water temperatures prevented organisms from any activity that would disturb the bottom and produce suspended particles. Small microscopic organisms were not abundant to cloud the water.

A movement caught my eye. At first, I thought it was the current causing the object to move, but then the objects began to move against the current. They looked like chunks of material from the stream bottom.

After considering the clues, I realized that I was watching caddisfly cases moving. Inside each case was a caddisfly larva with just its head and legs sticking out. The rest of its body was inside the case. If danger approaches, the head and legs are also tucked inside the case.

Caddisfly cases are marvels of construction. Upon hatching from an egg, the young caddisfly larvae begins the construction of its case. Each species builds a different kind of case. Several species can be seen in a stream or lake.

As the young caddisfly grows, it adds onto the case to accommodate its increasing size. Because they use debris from the stream bottom, the cases, and thus they themselves, are very well

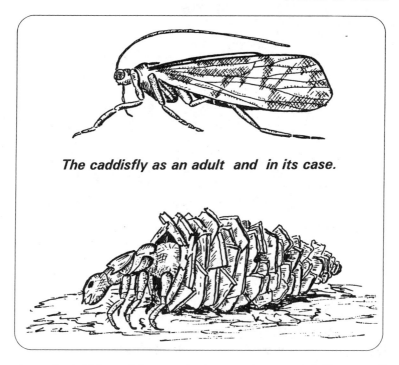

The caddisfly as an adult and in its case.

camouflaged. Most of the cases in the stream were made from small pieces of plant material stacked like a loaf of bread for a length of about one-half inch. Another species used hollow sections of aquatic plants. It was so large that three separate pieces, each a half-inch long, were connected together. Some species use only small grains of sand or pebbles, while others decorate their case with abandoned snail shells.

During summer the caddisfly larva will mature and transform into winged adults. Large numbers of these winged adults can be seen near the water where they emerged. People who flyfish are well aware of the caddisfly and their emergence from the aquatic stage of their life cycle.

Next time you pass by a clear stream, take the time to look carefully into the water and you may see caddisfly cases. If you can gently take one from the stream and examine it; you will be amazed at the architecture.

175

SWANS OF THE TUNDRA

One cold day in March I spotted a flock of 40 tundra swans flying overhead.

They were known as whistling swans for a long time, until recently it was discovered that they are a subspecies of a European swan, so they now refer to both species as tundra swans.

Tundra swans are one of three species of swan found in Michigan. Mute swans introduced from Europe have established themselves as breeding residents throughout much of Michigan. But as their name suggests, they rarely if ever call or vocalize when flying.

In the early 1990s, trumpeter swans were introduced into Michigan in an attempt to reestablish a species that was historically a resident in the Great Lakes region. Some birds were placed in Seney National Wildlife Refuge in Michigan's Upper Peninsula and some were placed in the Flat River State Game Area.

Since trumpeter swans are very rare, the group I heard calling overhead had to be tundra swans. If I had not heard them I would surely have missed seeing them. Their white bodies blended into the grayish overcast sky that day.

Although swans have been know to fly as high as 10,000 feet, these birds were probably just 1,000 feet overhead and flying 35 miles per hour.

Spring is when tundra swans migrate through our area from their wintering grounds on Chesapeake Bay to their nesting areas in northern Alaska and Canada. Thousands of swans rest in fields

Tundra swans in flight.

near Wallaceburg, Ontario, Canada, between legs of their journey.

This flock was heading southeast toward Lake St. Clair and open water, where small flocks regularly winter. As long as they can find open water to feed on aquatic plants, they will be able to survive the cold winter weather.

Trumpeter swans, found in Yellowstone National Park, spend the entire winter in ponds and lakes kept open by hot water from underground.

Opportunities to observe wildlife around cities are more numerous than you may think, but in order to see as much as possible, you have to keep all your senses attuned. Although looking up is not a common habit of human nature, it does expand the area in which wildlife can be seen.

177

THE EXCAVATOR OF YOUR LAWN
TUNNELLING MOLES

When I was a youngster, the only occupations I recall were a fireman, policeman, baker and doctor. Now I know that there are endless job titles and classifications in society. Each person has a specific job to do, and each person's job is necessary for the functioning of a system.

In the natural world, it's much the same way. Plants and animals have developed to survive in almost every conceivable place. Functioning systems have developed with producers, consumers and decomposers in forests, meadows, wetlands and deserts. All the components are needed in order for the system to function properly.

When exploring the various jobs and workers in natural systems, it is amazing to see the variety that has developed through the years. Bacteria survive in the hot springs of Yellowstone National Park and produce the various colors in the pools. Some insects spend their entire life in the upper branches of a tree. Other animals, like the emperor penguin, subsist in subzero temperatures of the Antarctic for nine weeks without eating.

Even the subterranean world is utilized by a mammal. Eastern moles are seldom visible, but evidence of their presence is frequently seen.

Both the eastern and star-nosed mole are well adapted for

tunneling through soil. They have soft, dense fur that lies flat comfortably, no matter which direction they travel in their confined tunnels. Their front feet are flattened like shovels. Even their nails are flattened for digging.

A mild December in 1988 had yet to freeze the soil, which explains why I was still able to see new excavations from moles as I walked through the woods. Later, when the ground froze, moles spent their time in deeper tunnels and dens.

Shallow tunnels just under the ground are frequently used for feeding. Earthworms, grubs, insects and other small invertebrates make up 80 percent of a mole's diet. They must eat one-third their weight (2-4 oz.) each day.

FORTUNATELY, MOLES ARE SOLITARY ANIMALS. SEVERAL TUNNELS IN A LAWN MAY BE THE WORK OF JUST ONE OR TWO INDIVIDUALS.

Sharp, pointed teeth the length of the skull are used for crushing and eating the hard exoskeleton of insects. Such teeth aren't useful for eating plant material.

Home owners with mole problems don't have to worry about their eating the grass; they are looking for grubs and insects under the lawn. Though their tunnels may look unsightly in a well manicured lawn, if the grub problem is cured then the mole problem should go away. Fortunately, moles are solitary animals. Several tunnels in a lawn may be the work of just one or two individuals.

The role a mole plays in the natural world is just one of many niches or jobs that animals perform to keep the system going.

The Sounds Of Flight

Our sense of hearing is stimulated constantly. So much so that we tend not to listen to many sounds. Background noises of traffic, voices, humming electric motors and such are frequently ignored.

Walking through the woods and meadows can also stimulate your sense of hearing, but with totally different sounds. Wind rustling leaves, birds singing, bees humming or frogs calling are sounds likely to be heard because they are so different from the usual sounds of the city.

These and other sounds are produced in a variety of ways. One sound that I am always intrigued by is that produced by the wing feathers of birds. I remember sitting in my grandfather's woods watching for squirrels, and any other activity, when all of a sudden I heard a *whssss whsss whssss* sound. When I looked around to see what was creating such a sound, I saw my first pileated wood-pecker.

Waterfowl enthusiasts can identify when certain ducks known as common goldeneye are approaching by listening to the whistling of their wings. Feathers cutting through the wind act like the reed of a woodwind instrument and create a vibration. Not all birds have the proper feather structure or flight manner to produce such loud sounds. Mourning doves flying to and from your yard produce sound in a similar manner.

Owls have a fringe on the leading edge of their wing feathers. This fringe prevents any vibration caused by wind through the

A common Snipe.

feathers. Though nights are not always quiet, owls do not want to be heard by mice or any other potential prey.

A walk through many woodlots in the midwest during spring might allow one to hear the low thumping of the ruffed grouse. Males select a fallen log, or stump, on which to perform their courtship ritual. Once in position, the male stands upright and flaps its wings toward its body. It does not slap its body, it compresses the air to make the sound. Each session starts slow and gets faster and faster. This sound is almost felt more than it is heard.

Common snipe found in wetland areas have interesting shaped tail feathers which they use to produce a courtship sound. The low whinnowing sound is produced when the bird dives in an undulating flight. Wind passing through the spread tail feathers produces this eerie sound.

Outdoor experiences can be stimulating to all the senses if you condition yourself to using them.

Backing Up The Eyes

In the age of computers one of the first things we learn to do is back up data on a regular basis. That is because there is always the chance that something may happen to the main system.

Animals exhibit this same approach to help them survive in the wild. Owls, for instance, have very good eye sight. Their eyes are also very big. Some species of owl have eyes as large as that of man. Large eyes provide large pupil openings which allow what faint light is still available to reach the back of the eye.

But if there is no light, no animal can see, no matter how large their eye is. When lights are turned off inside a cave it is impossible for any animal to see anything.

So owls and other nocturnal animals rely on backup "systems" to be used when light is not available. In the case of owls, they have excellent hearing. Asymmetrical ear openings enable owls to locate their prey very accurately, because sound does not hit each ear at the same time. A slight delay between sound perception in each ear allows an owl to locate their prey in total darkness.

A slight delay between sound perception in each ear allows an owl to locate their prey in total darkness.

Other animals that live in total darkness also use a backup system. Two cave dwelling birds use an echo location system like bats. They make a sound that bounces off objects and is heard by the bird, thus enabling them to avoid objects even in total darkness. Outside the cave they use their eyes.

Bats, by the way, are not blind, as some old stories proclaim, but they cannot see very well. Since most of their activities are conducted in darkness, they have developed an echo location system that enables them to function.

One small mammal known as a star-nosed mole has poor eyesight also, but has a sense that most other animals lack. Finger-like projections from the nose of a star-nosed mole are able to detect minute electrical charges from the muscles of their potential prey.

Perceiving the environment is essential for any animal. Fortunately, most animals have at least five ways to do so in case one or two are insufficient.

A Gnaw For Each Species
Nut Crunch

Sometimes the most simple things are overlooked and taken for granted. For instance, people in the civilized world eat food with utensils. Those utensils vary depending on the culture. Chopsticks are used in oriental countries and knives and forks by western countries.

But even people who use knives and forks use them in different ways. Europeans often hold their fork in their left hand and retain the knife in their right for cutting. Americans, on the other hand, switch their fork back to their right hand after they have finished cutting with their knife.

So it should not be a great surprise to know that animals eat their food in different ways, and that they must learn how to eat.

Squirrels that we see in our backyards must learn how to open a nut in an efficient manner. They automatically gnaw at it and eventually extract the meat from the inside, but after practicing, they learn how to extract the nut meat more effectively.

Close examination reveals that not all squirrels open their nuts in the same way. Large squirrels, such as gray squirrels, have jaws strong enough to snap off chunks of shell with their lower incisors after they gnawed a hole in the shell.

Red squirrels, or the "fur-rari" racing through your yard and branches, are smaller, and open acorns in a different manner. Like the racing car, a "fur-rari" has a black "racing" stripe that separates

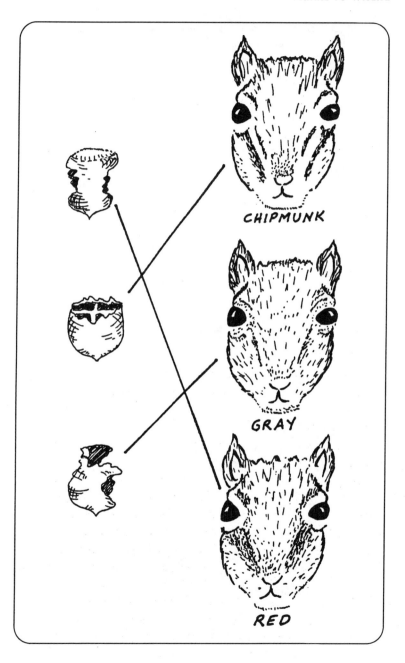

CHIPMUNK

GRAY

RED

its reddish brown back from its white belly. It also has a white ring around the eye, reminiscent of a headlight on a racing car. Its reddish color is also similar to that of the racing car.

Discarded shells from the red squirrel show they have gnawed openings on opposite sides of the acorn. They look as though a person took a single large bite from opposite sides of an apple.

Smaller squirrels, like the chipmunk and the flying squirrel, clean out the meat like we clean a pumpkin. They remove the top third of the shell in order to get inside.

Examining the shell remains of feeding areas along fence rows, or on favorite logs, may reveal who had come to dinner.

Fox Sparrows

Once you become aware of the usual things around you, then unusual or incongruous things stand out.

People who have been watching birds for a few years know those species that are likely to be seen in our area at a particular time of the year. Some visitors, like the tree sparrow, are seen only during the winter. Observing one during July would be most unusual.

Fox sparrows, not usually seen in our area during winter, are good sightings. They are a large, gray-brown sparrow with a heavily streaked breast. In the center of the breast, several streaks form a spot, like that of the song sparrow.

In addition to its large size, it has a reddish tail - hence the name "fox." Before common names for birds were standardized, they were called foxy finch, fox-tail and fox colored sparrow.

Earthy red coloration and size are physical features that make this species distinct, but so is its behavior. At the feeder, it is one of only a few species that scrapes the ground with both feet at the same time in a hopping motion. This short, jumping behavior is used to unearth seeds covered by snow and soil.

Typically this bird winters south of Ohio. But maybe attractive feeding stations along its fall migration route from northern Canada make wintering in the Great Lakes area possible.

During the December 20, 1988 Detroit Audubon Society Christmas Bird Count four fox sparrows were counted. That was only the second time they had been recorded in the 43-year history of the count. Prior to that, only one bird was seen in 1975.

Careful observation of nature at various times of the year can provide new and different rewards. I had the good fortune to became familiar with the fox sparrow on its breeding ground near Hudson Bay. Its beautiful ringing song was new to me, but very enjoyable to hear while walking through the muskeg.

Since most people cannot see them on their breeding grounds, it's nice that some will visit you right in your own backyard, if you take the time to look carefully.

AT THE FEEDER, A FOX SPARROW IS ONE OF A FEW SPECIES THAT SCRAPES THE GROUND WITH BOTH FEET AT THE SAME TIME IN A HOPPING MOTION.

The Author

Exploring natural areas over the years has provided Timothy Nowicki with many opportunities to experience the wonders of nature. Childhood outings primed him for his master's degree from Central Michigan University, while additional studies at the University of Minnesota and Eastern Michigan University helped to solidify his biological and educational training.

Nowicki has been on the board of directors of the Detroit Audubon Society for the last nine years. He teaches nature classes at several Detroit area facilities, including Schoolcraft College. In the mid-1980s, Nowicki co-authored and illustrated two guides on bird identification and while at the University of Minnesota he wrote and directed production of the *Uncle Fogy Bird Songs* cassette tape. He has also contributed articles to *Michigan Natural Resources* magazine and *Seasons*.

In 1984 Nowicki began writing and illustrating a nature column for the Observer & Eccentric newspapers and since 1987 he has been a weekly guest naturalist on the Jimmy Launce Show on WJR radio. More recently Nowicki has been hosting a cable television program entitled *Animal Club*.

In 1989, Nowicki was honored by the Michigan Audubon Society for his articles in the Observer & Eccentric newspapers. He received the Russell Bengel Award from the Michigan Wildlife Habitat Foundation and has been honored by the National Audubon Society.

Nowicki is currently a naturalist at Independence Oaks Nature Center, operated by the Oakland County Parks and Recreation Commission.